HEIR APPARENT

The author

HEIR APPARENT
An Autobiography

KARAN SINGH

DELHI
OXFORD UNIVERSITY PRESS
BOMBAY CALCUTTA MADRAS
1982

Oxford University Press, Walton Street, Oxford OX2 6DP

LONDON GLASGOW NEW YORK TORONTO
DELHI BOMBAY CALCUTTA MADRAS KARACHI
KUALA LUMPUR SINGAPORE HONG KONG TOKYO
NAIROBI DAR ES SALAAM CAPE TOWN
MELBOURNE AUCKLAND
and associates in
BEIRUT BERLIN IBADAN MEXICO CITY

Printed in India by P. K. Ghosh
at Eastend Printers, 3 Dr Suresh Sarkar Road, Calcutta 700 014
and published by R. Dayal, Oxford University Press,
2/11 Ansari Road, Daryaganj, New Delhi 110 002

For
Vikram and Ajay
heirs apparent to the future

Be not parted—growing old, taking thought, thriving together, moving under a common bond, speaking sweetly to one another, have one aim and be of one mind.

Atharva Veda III. 30. 5

Preface

Twenty-two years is a rather brief span for an autobiography, but my early life was subject to so many unusual circumstances that the reader may find something of interest in this story of a boy growing to manhood between two worlds. I have closed this volume with the dramatic political events in 1953 following my election as 'Sadar-i-Riyasat' of Jammu and Kashmir the previous year.

Soon after I began writing this work, I discovered that the venture was not without hazards. Recollections of early childhood are generally hazy with a few clear patches, while as time advances the whole situation becomes increasingly complex and to that extent more difficult to record adequately. However, I found the exercise in introspection valuable and fascinating, as it forced me to look backwards into time and space and, inevitably, inwards into myself.

I have been greatly aided in reconstructing my early years by the fact that my father was meticulous in maintaining files of correspondence. After he passed away, a number of these came into my possession, including all my letters to him, copies of his replies as well as a number of important files containing his correspondence with the Government of India after 1947. For my part, I adopted his practice and maintained copies of all important letters that I wrote and received. In the later chapters of this book I have quoted at some length from these documents, particularly from the large number of letters written to me by my political guru, Jawaharlal Nehru.

I am grateful to my daughter Jyotsna Chauhan and to my editor at the Oxford University Press for reading through the typescript and making useful suggestions; and to my wife for helping me select the portfolio of photographs. The Jammu and Kashmir Government was good enough to allow me to consult some of the files in its archives pertaining to my birth and early years.

It is a matter of personal regret that Sheikh Abdullah passed away shortly before the publication of this book. Despite our sharp political differences during and after the period covered by this volume, we retained cordial personal relations till the end. There is no doubt that he was one of the tallest Kashmiris, both literally and figuratively, and that he made a unique contribution to the development of the Kashmiri people over the last half century. His role in opposing communal forces during the turbulent years of Partition will long be remembered.

I have dedicated this book to my sons who, while growing up in a very different atmosphere to the one I encountered in my childhood, will none the less have to face a world changing even more rapidly than it was then. 'Samyak samsarati iti samsara'— that which constantly changes is the world, as the ancient Sanskrit has it. Or, as John Masefield put it,

> Out of the earth of rest or range
> Perpetual in perpetual change,
> The unknown passing through the strange.

And yet it is this very change that lends excitement to the adventure of living, zest to the intellectual inquiry after truth and challenge to the unending spiritual quest. For it has rightly been said that behind the ever-changing world lies an eternal reality, and it is my belief that the true destiny of man lies in discovering that reality, comprehending it and, finally, becoming a part of its infinite dimensions. And so I like to look upon this story of my early years as the opening of a quest for a yet dimly perceived goal, the beginning of a journey to a yet unknown destination.

KARAN SINGH

27 October 1982

Contents

Plates

Chapter 1

The resort town of Cannes on the Mediterranean was always a favourite haunt of high society—European and, in other times, Indian. Among the several notable tourist establishments built along the famous Cote d'azur is the Hotel Martinez. Early in 1931 the dashing and handsome Maharaja of Jammu and Kashmir, Sir Hari Singh, and his lovely wife, Maharani Tara Devi, checked into the entire third floor of the hotel. The Maharaja was representing the Indian Princes at the Round Table Conference held in London that year. But London in the winter was foggy and unpleasant, while Cannes was glorious, with lots of polo and champagne and the balmy breeze from the Mediterranean so greatly prized by an aristocracy sublimely unaware that its days throughout the world were rapidly drawing to a close.

The Hotel Martinez still stands, a square, handsome structure commanding a fine view of the Mediterranean. In the northern corner of the third floor in suite 318–19–20 the young Maharani was in an advanced stage of pregnancy. She was only twenty-one, and was attended upon by a bevy of maid servants, some from India and others from France, for in those days servants in Europe were still in the realm of the possible. There were last minute complications, labour pains were unduly delayed, the maid servants, the Maharaja's personal physician Colonel J. H. Hugo and the eminent obstetrician Sir Henry Simson worked round the clock, while the Maharaja with his friends and staff was playing polo during the day and drinking champagne deep into the night. At last the appointed hour struck; on the ninth of March 1931 I came into the world this time round, nine pounds in weight and bawling vigorously. The odyssey had begun.

My birth was greeted with extravagant enthusiasm by the people of Jammu and Kashmir, irrespective of religion, caste or creed. Partly this was because the princely order in India still had some glory, and the birth of a Yuvaraj (heir apparent) was always a matter for rejoicing. But in my case the causes appear to have been deeper. My father had ascended the throne in 1925 on the passing away of his uncle, Maharaja Pratap Singh, who had ruled the State for forty years. During that time the British, alarmed at the growing power of the Russian Empire, had moved to consolidate their grip over the strategic northern provinces of Gilgit and Skardu. These were contiguous to the Russian Empire and had been added to the State of Jammu and Kashmir by the vision of Maharaja Gulab Singh and the military genius of his great generals, led by Wazir Zorawar Singh. Indeed, during Maharaja Pratap Singh's reign the British Political Department had worked up an elaborate intrigue to depose him on the grounds of alleged collusion with a 'foreign power', and had in fact obliged him to surrender power to a Council of Regency. He might have been actually deposed, but the plot was revealed by the *Amrita Bazar Patrika* of Calcutta in a celebrated article entitled 'Condemned Unheard'. This caused a furore in the British Parliament and the Political Office had to back down.

My father had married thrice earlier, twice in Saurashtra and once in the neighbouring hill State of Chamba, but his first wife had died with a child still in her womb, and the other two marriages were childless. People had begun to fear that if there was no heir to the throne, my father himself was an only child, the almighty Viceroy would one day invoke the notorious doctrine of lapse and take the State over under direct British administration. Thus when my father decided to marry once again—this time a girl from a remote village on the banks of the river Beas in Kangra district of the old Panjab—fresh hopes were raised. And when it was rumoured that the new Maharani was expecting a child, excitement began to mount.

My father's decision to take my mother to Europe for the delivery was variously interpreted. Some felt that he was doing this to keep the mother and child away from the malevolent machinations of the *zenana*, the female household where dozens of Maharanis, Ranis, ladies-in-waiting and maid servants lived —relics of previous rulers. Others assumed that France had been chosen because there the agents of the ubiquitous British Empire, upon whom at that time the sun never set, would not be able to operate. In all events, the birth of the Yuvaraj, if contemporary records and accounts are to be believed, triggered off an almost delirious wave of enthusiasm among the people of the State. There were official proclamations. The slaughter of animals, fishing and shooting were prohibited for three days, the 10th, 11th and 12th of March, and these were declared public holidays in the State. Offerings were made in temples, mosques and gurudwaras, and all school children were given sweets and asked to pray for the long life of the prince. I still meet people in the most unlikely places who remember having received the sweets as children. The announcement of my birth was made in Srinagar by the Army and Public Works Minister, General Janak Singh, while in Jammu this was done by Mr Wakefield, one of my father's Ministers.

General Janak Singh recorded a brief note on 17 March which contains the following paragraph:

The 9th March was the first bright day when the weather in Kashmir cleared after a long spell of bad winter. It was on this day that the newspapers containing the happy news of the Gandhi–Irwin agreement reached Srinagar. The people of Kashmir thought these happenings a good omen and believed that the future destiny of the Prince was bright.

After spending six weeks in Cannes the whole party sailed back to India on the *Kaiser-i-Hind*, a P & O steamship, which docked in Bombay at the end of April 1931. It was thus Bombay, not Kashmir, that was my first point of contact with India and, strangely enough, Bombay was also to play an important part in my life for the next thirty years. A large group of officials and courtiers from Jammu and Kashmir had assembled at the Gateway of India to welcome my father, along with a number of ruling princes. Among the latter, as my father subsequently was fond of recounting, was the late Maharaja Ganga Singhji of Bikaner. Apparently I took one look at his famous moustache and set up a loud yell which subsided only when he finally left the cabin. There were also the late Nawab Taley Mohammad Khan of Palanpur, a close friend of my father, after whom our Srinagar house was named, and the 'Nightingale of India', Sarojini Naidu. From Bombay the party went by train to Jammu where on 3 May a triumphal reception awaited us. My father and mother went through the town in an open horse carriage, while I was driven behind in a car along with my English nurse Miss Doris Tranchell. Then, after five days, the whole performance was repeated in Srinagar. From the files and numerous people I have met who were present, it is clear that for days there was a staggering array of feasts, receptions, banquets, illuminations, free cinema shows, music performances, the distribution of sweets and sundry festivities. My formal naming ceremony was performed on 11 May, and Mr Wakefield solemnly announced that I would be called 'Shree Yuvaraj Karan Singhji Bahadur'.

Historically, this could perhaps be described as the zenith of Dogra rule in Jammu and Kashmir. Almost immediately after the festivities were concluded the State was plunged into serious political turmoil, after which things were never again to be the same. Oddly enough, my birth coincided with the emergence of a hitherto obscure schoolteacher into the political life of the State, with repercussions that continue down to the present day. His name—Sheikh Mohammed Abdullah. One theory is that the disturbances and the Sheikh's activities were in fact master-minded by the British, both because my birth had upset their 'doctrine of lapse' policy, and also to teach my father a lesson for having made at the Round Table Conference earlier that year a remarkably patriotic speech urging the British to respect the aspirations of the Indian people. He had said in the course of his speech that 'as Indians and loyal to the land whence they derived their birth and infant nurture, the Princes stood solidly as the rest of their countrymen for India's enjoyment of a position of honour and equality in the British Commonwealth of Nations'.

Be that as it may, from as far back as I can remember, I have been regaled with glowing accounts of the festivities and cele-brations that followed my birth, coupled occasionally with unusually mysterious astrological predictions regarding my future life. After a while I began to wonder whether what I did with my life would in fact justify the joy and expectations that my arrival appeared to have elicited. If even a fraction of the people who rejoiced had done so from feelings deeper than formal loyalty, it was a debt that would have to be repaid in full measure in the years and decades ahead.

Looking through the yellowing files I find that all the religious ceremonies connected with my childhood were performed with the meticulous attention to detail that was characteristic of my father. Programmes were neatly printed, and every feature clearly spelt out down to the minutest item. The *Annaprashan* (cereal tasting) ceremony was held on 8 February 1932 and the *Mundan* (tonsure) on 7 December 1933. Every year until 1947 my birthday was treated as a public holiday; a salute of 17 guns would be fired from all forts; shooting, fishing and the killing of animals were prohibited; prisoners were released; alms distributed to the poor and all palaces and public buildings in Srinagar and Jammu illuminated. Religious ceremonies were held to which I was taken, attended by my father, mother and other relatives.

My earliest recollections are of looking up at the sky outside Amar Mahal, our mini-castle in Jammu which is now a museum and library, with someone pointing out an eagle to me, a tiny black speck against the unending blue vastness; and later, a curiously vivid memory of looking at myself in a mirror in a smaller building within the same campus, almost as if I was seeing myself for the first time. At the age of three I was taken away from my mother and an independent establishment set up for me in separate houses, at Srinagar in summer and Jammu in winter. I was allowed to see my mother every day for only one hour, and my father thrice a week. This was obviously not an ideal family environment, and it flowed from a deep incompatibility between my parents. My mother was a village girl from Kangra; my father was the ruler of the largest of India's over five hundred native States. My mother was deeply religious; my father remained till the end of his days a virtual agnostic. My mother was warm, gregarious and loved children; my father was stern, severe and moved only in a carefully chosen circle of courtiers and very few friends. My mother was strong on conversation; my father was so formidable that normal conversation in his presence was virtually impossible; my mother was superstitious, demonstrative, emotional; my father was neat, meticulous, aloof. This psychological and emotional imbalance led to a good deal of tension and mutual conflict.

Understandably, my early sympathy lay almost entirely with my mother. I cherished the visits to her, while she doted on me and would count the hours for me to appear. She resented my having been taken away from her on the grounds that she would spoil me, and was often in tears when my allotted hour was over. For many years the knowledge of her distress made me deeply unhappy, and I would often lie awake at night crying softly, thinking of her. She was beautiful, with large, expressive eyes which, as a friend of my father used to say, she knew how to use. To me, of course, she was for years the epitome of grace and love. When I was brought to her she would first take me to her prayer-room where she would put flowers and a few coins into my hands, to be offered to the various pictures of gods and goddesses installed there. Then we would sit and play games with her maid servants, or with her nieces and nephews, my only relatives of comparable age, as there were no close relations on my father's side of the family.

Sometimes in the mellow Jammu evenings we would all assemble on the large veranda in Amar Mahal with its magnificent view of the Shivalik range, the triple-peaked mountains of Vaishno Devi dominating the skyline and the river Tawi winding down to the plains. There, the small earthen lamps were lit, and with my mother in the lead we would all walk round the sacred *tulasi* (basil) plant grown in an earthen pot, singing devotional songs in our lilting mother tongue, Dogri. Years later I translated one of those songs dedicated to the great Mother of Radiances:

O Mother Jwala, dwelling amidst the mountains,
fulfil our innermost desires.
A bright red garment adorns your body
and on your forehead is the yellow saffron mark,
the five-hued shawl covers your head,
its edges shimmering with golden embroidery,
O Mother Jwala, dwelling amidst the mountains,
fulfil our innermost desires.

From all corners of the earth, O Mother,
pilgrims come and sing thy praises,
having bowed before thy shrine
all their cravings are satisfied,
O Mother Jwala, dwelling amidst the mountains,
fulfil our innermost desires.

Brahma, the Creator, recites the Vedas before thee
and Shankar meditates upon thee amidst the mountains;

the devotee who sings thy praises
is granted by thee his heart's desire,
O Mother Jwala, dwelling amidst the mountains,
fulfil our innermost desires.

Although I did not then understand the full meaning of the words, the rhythmic mingling of the sacred and the mundane, of the here and the hereafter, had a deep effect upon me. My mother loved folk music. She had a powerful voice and would sing for hours with the *dholki* (two-faced drum), in chorus with her maids and other female relatives and ladies from the city who visited her. Evidently I developed my permanent romance with music from these early childhood memories of Dogra–Pahari songs, because for the rest of my life music has been a predominant motif in my consciousness.

While the daily, and later only thrice-weekly, visits to my mother were eagerly awaited, the meetings with my father were a source of awe. He was affectionate enough, without being demonstrative, and always carried my photograph in his gold cigarette case. But his whole presence and reputation were so formidable that it was difficult to think of anything to say. The joyful spontaneity of the visits to my mother was lacking, and it was only many years later that I began to realize that my father's forbidding exterior was really something of a protective armour that he had developed through the circumstances of his own life. An only child, brought up in a cloak and dagger atmosphere of court and family intrigue, he must have been through a traumatic situation before he grew to manhood. And soon thereafter, on his first visit to England, he became the unfortunate victim of a vicious blackmail plot that brought him a great deal of undeserved censure. By the time I was born my father was thirty-six and had been on the throne for six years. He always took a close and careful interest in the way I was brought up, but being by nature undemonstrative his relationship with me never became as free as my relationship with my mother. There was a brief period when it might have flowered, but destiny and the inexorable thrust of history intervened to thwart this.

Chapter 2

Along with a separate establishment consisting of about fifteen employees, I was looked after by a series of British guardians until I went to public school at the age of eleven. The earliest was a Mrs Wyndham, whose husband, Colonel Wyndham, was Assistant Resident. I remember her only as an elderly woman with a broad hat, and recall the Colonel once giving me an empty metal cigar box lined with crackling aluminium foil, silver on one side and bright red on the other. After the Wyndhams came the Ritchies. He had been a master in Mayo College, Ajmer and was evidently Scottish, because my only clear recollection is of his teaching us some charming Scottish folk tunes and marching songs. Mrs Ritchie was a bit of a dragon whom all of us, including her husband, treated with rather nervous respect.

At about this time, around 1935 when I was four, two companions came to live with me, sons of Rajput courtiers close to my father. They were Digvijay Singh ('Digby'), who was the son of Rao Bahadur Kartar Singh, a senior and shrewd administrator who played an important role in the administration of the State; and Digpal Singh ('Bilti'), whose father, Major Faqir Singh, was for many years my father's favourite staff officer. When they came to live with me I was repeatedly told of my father's rather un-Christian instructions that if I ever slapped them once they should respond by slapping me twice. As it turned out the admonition was unnecessary; they were both older and stronger than I and the occasion to implement the instructions never arose.

By then I had acquired the nickname 'Tiger'. Apparently one day I crawled into the room where my father and his close friend, the ruler of Jodhpur, Maharaja Umaid Singhji, were seated. Umaid Singhji said that I was on all fours like a tiger, and the name stuck. My father and his friends invariably referred to me as Tiger, and years later Jawaharlal Nehru and others of his generation did the same. It is an odd coincidence that decades later I was called upon to head Project Tiger, designed to save this magnificent animal from extinction, and also that as Chairman of the Indian Board for Wildlife I was responsible for making the tiger India's national animal in place of the lion.

The three of us—Tiger, Digby and Bilti—lived together for several years in a world of our own. In Srinagar we were at the lovely cottage on Shankaracharya Hill, then known as Taley Manzil after Taley Mohammad Khan of Palanpur, a close friend of my father, which commands a fantastic double view. On one side is the Dal Lake behind which towers a range of high, bare mountains with the peak of Harmukh, eternally capped with snow, peeping over their shoulders; while on the other side the entire sweep of the snowy Pir Panjal range stretches from Gulmarg in the east to Banihal in the west. In Jammu we lived in a small building known as Karan Niwas, originally a staff house attached to one of the larger palaces in the estate. There was a full complement of servants with whom we played football, while my father's Goan butlers (Fernandez, Lobo, D'Souza) came down occasionally to play badminton. We had a strict regimen, dietary, academic and recreational. We were not allowed any Indian food or sweets, and therefore had to make do with the English food which the guardian of the moment and his wife relished. Tea was our best meal, for which there were buttered scones and sponge fingers, delicious short-bread made by Huntley and Palmers, and the inevitable sandwiches served on silver dishes. Indeed, breakfast and tea were the only meals in which the English culinary genius (such as it was) seemed capable of any sort of coherent expression.

For our studies we had an Indian tutor, Amar Nath Khosla, who taught us English, mathematics and other subjects. He had a neat handwriting, and every month would prepare a meti-culous report on the three of us, covering our studies, games and general behaviour, which went to the guardian and, through him, to my father. It was Masterji, as we called him, who one day brought us a black marble tablet with the figure of a frail, dhoti-clad man inlaid in mother-of-pearl. This, he said, was Gandhiji, the great leader of India. But he only showed it to us and did not leave it with us for fear that he would get into serious trouble with the guardian. We were also initiated into the evocative if somewhat inelegant gibe that if all Indians were to urinate together it would be enough to wash all the Britishers in India into the sea. For some reason the three of us were anti-British, though we never showed this openly. I distinctly remember listening to the radio in September 1939, when I was eight and a half years old, and hearing the news that the Second World War had broken out. Thereafter we were all secretly rooting for the Germans, and would jump around gleefully whenever there was news of British reverses. Only one servant, Raghunath Singh, would infuriate us by insisting that the British would never be defeated despite initial setbacks. We would all taunt him, but he stuck imperturbably to his guns, Churchillian in his supreme confidence of ultimate victory. I discovered later that he had been for some time in one of the regiments of the Indian Army.

The Ritchies were in due course succeeded by Captain and Mrs Wreford, who turned out to be our favourites among the British. Captain (Reggie) Wreford, formerly Census Commissioner in the State, had lost an arm in the First World War, but he used his stump to astonishing effect and was an excellent shot. Katherine Wreford was a woman of charm and quiet efficiency and their children, Joan and Douglas, both considerably older than us, were at school in England and came out every year on their holidays. During the Wreford tenure we started learning badminton, tennis, football and hockey. We were also initiated into cricket, and would write letters to Bradman and Hammond and other such legendary heroes. Despite this, cricket did not become one of my favourite games, and I have never had more than a desultory interest in this curiously protracted sport. Occasionally we were allowed to go shopping, usually in Gulmarg which at that time had glittering shops filled with the latest foreign products to cater to the large number of British people who flocked there in the summer. During the winter, when in Jammu, our shopping consisted of regular fortnightly trips with our guardian to Sialkot, only an hour's drive away. There we would have tea at Ghulam Qadir's, a department store, and buy comics from a small corner bookshop opposite. We also subscribed to three comics from England—*Tiger Tim* (mine), *Donald Duck* (Digby's) and *Puck* (Bilti's).

My father was an excellent rider and, while he was too heavy to be really top-class, he reached the respectable handicap of five in polo. He was keen that I should become a great polo player, and from the age of three I was forced to ride almost every day of my life, beginning on a box saddle and a tiny horse and gradually moving on to larger animals. I had several falls, and on one terrifying occasion my horse bolted in the Jammu pologround and I hung on to it, petrified, until it finally exhausted itself and came to a halt. During those years I saw some of the finest polo in the world as the famed Jaipur team with the remarkable combined handicap of 35 (out of a possible maximum of 40) would come up to Srinagar every year. We would watch the game from the special Zenana pavilion along with my mother, my grandmother and other elderly ladies in white. These were among the few occasions when I met our elderly female relatives, though every two or three months my mother would take me to the Zenana palaces to visit them.

An event I remember was the great Quetta earthquake in May 1935. For weeks we were not allowed to spend the night inside Taley Manzil and, to our great excitement, had to sleep out in the garden. Also, there was the occasion when my tonsils had to be removed. A room in Karan Niwas at Jammu was converted into an operating theatre, and the well-known surgeon, Colonel Harper Nelson, came over from Lahore to do the operation. I remember struggling with horror under the chloroform mask held over my face and, later, my father paying one of his rare visits to me and sitting on my bed with a jigsaw puzzle, pleasantly surprised that I was eating ice cream because it was supposed to be good for my post-operative throat.

Apart from the fact that my first contact with Indian soil took place in Bombay, that great city became an important venue for my early experiences. Though in his early life an avid polo player, my father later took to racing in a big way and this inevitably led him to Bombay which had the best racing in India. Consequently, while he spent the six summer months in Srinagar, in the winters he would spend only about two months in Jammu and four in Bombay. The first time we went to Bombay, in 1940, he stayed in a rented building called Nishat House on Carmichael Road. All I can recall of that visit is that we used to get a delicious orange drink called Pure Gold, sipped luxuriously through straws, and also that the day before we left the three of us were roundly reprimanded for having ruined our sitting-room by spilling ink all over the sofas and carpet. The next year my father shifted to a block of flats he bought at 94 Nepean Sea Road. He lived on the top floor, the sixth, and for me he kept the first floor which had a terrace garden—a novelty in those days.

We lived there for some months with our guardian. By then the British guardians had been dispensed with, and Colonel Kailash Narayan Haksar appointed in their place. It was an open secret that my father wanted him as political adviser, and adopted the somewhat transparent stratagem of appointing him guardian to the Heir Apparent. This highlighted a strange tendency in my father that was ultimately to prove his political undoing—his inability to trust anyone for any length of time. He selected his Prime Ministers with great care, but no sooner had he appointed one than he would begin cultivating someone else as a sort of counterbalance. With the exception of N. Gopalaswami Ayyangar, who was Prime Minister of the State for six years from 1934 to 1939, this happened with all the succeeding incumbents—Raja Maharaj Singh; B. N. Rau; Colonel K. N. Haksar; Pandit Ramchandra Kak and General Janak Singh—right down to the crisis of 1947.

Colonel Haksar was a large man with bushy eyebrows, gold-rimmed spectacles and a military limp which combined to give him a formidable appearance. But despite his stern exterior he was fond of me, and would often seat me on his knee with great affection. My father, I suspect, was a trifle scared of him too, and though he joked about him with us in his absence, he was discreet when 'Colonel Sahib' was in the room. Colonel Haksar, in turn, while loyal to my father, by no means approved of all that he did. I remember him telling me one day with more than a touch of asperity as we drove away from a meeting with my father, 'Tiger, look very carefully, so that when you grow up you will know what *not* to do.' Colonel Haksar's eldest daughter Shyama Wattal had a marvellous way with children, and at her coaxing I wrote my first 'book', an eight-page, handwritten collection of poems and mini-essays.

It was in Bombay in 1940 that I was sent to my first school— the Cathedral High School—along with Digby and Bilti. At that time the school catered predominantly to English, Parsi and Anglo-Indian boys, and we were known as Singh I, Singh II and Singh III. These peculiar appellations became a bit of a bore, and although I went back for one more summer term the next year, I cannot say that I really derived any substantial benefit from that estimable institution. Piloo Mody, who was also at the Doon School when I went there later, has recorded that Zulfikar Ali Bhutto was his classmate at Cathedral, which means that we must have been there at the same time, although I do not remember Bhutto at school. The teachers were all English, even the Urdu ('Oordoo') teacher, who didn't seem to be able to speak a coherent sentence of that beautiful language himself.

Apart from some fellow princes, my father's friends were drawn largely from racing circles, but there was a small group of foreigners whom I remember vividly. Victor Rosenthal, a French jeweller who had enjoyed a fabulously chequered and romantic career, making and losing many fortunes *en route*, was a fascinating man with a chiselled beard and a warm temperament. He had known my father for decades, and handled much of his jewellery and foreign investments. He was a regular visitor to Kashmir in the summers, and always brought me lovely presents—books by Maupassant and O. Henry which I devoured with relish, a set of plastic hairbrushes, boxes of Swiss chocolates. I have described him as French simply because he lived in Paris and we all thought that was his nationality. It was only many years later that I discovered he was, in fact, Russian, having moved out—complete with beard—at roughly the same time as Lenin moved in. Freddie and Beryl Stileman, an English couple, were good friends of my parents. He was in the British firm of Killick Nixons, while Beryl was a woman of great beauty and vivacity. Almost exactly my father's age, she was the only person I remember who could tease him and speak quite naturally to him, a feat which in those days was looked upon as bordering on the supernatural.

Among the Indians, M. H. Ahmedbhoy and his wife Rukhsana were frequent visitors, not only because of his racing background but also because he was a superb singer. Despite exaggerated gestures as he sang, 'Mahmood Seth' was one of the finest amateurs I have ever heard. *Thumries* were his forte, and along with him my father frequently organized music parties where some of the best artists in India would perform, among them Kesarbai Kerkar, Siddheshwari Bai, Begum Akhtar and Meneka Shirodkar. My father did not sing himself, but he had a fine ear for good singing. It was at about this time that he got me to start learning classical music, an act for which I will remain eternally indebted to him. My first teacher was Balram Singh Rawat from the Nepal Terai. No great musician, he was a competent teacher and within a couple of years I had picked up several ragas. Ustad Vilayat Husain of the famous Agra gharana came to coach me for two summers. About three years later my father had HMV make some records (78 rpm) of my songs for private circulation, which he proudly sent round to his friends.

Music has remained one of the major forces in my life. The very first tune I can remember goes back to when I was four or five; a popular devotional ditty in praise of the boy-God Krishna, 'Sunā de, sunā de, sunā de Krishna, tū bānsuri dī tāan sunā de Krishna'. Some years later a new cinema hall opened in Srinagar called the Amrish Theatre (the owner, Pandit Krishan Bal, had wanted to name it after me but my father refused him permission. He therefore named it after his youngest son). I went with my parents to the opening, for which the celebrated dancer and actress Sadhona Bose had come all the way from Calcutta. As far as I can recall, her dancing on that occasion consisted largely of striking a variety of sculpturesque poses, scantily attired, upon a huge drum. However, there was another dance in which a man dressed in blue (the ocean) and a girl in green (a river) did a charming little number. The tune is one that will remain with me as long as I live. It was in the pentatonic raga, Bhupali. As soon as I heard that tune it was as if in some curious way a fountain had been released within me and the music seemed to pour out of my finger tips. For weeks the flow of those fine notes coursed through my veins. Later I learnt from Balram Singh several songs in this raga, as also in two other ragas equally wondrous— Durga and Malkauns. Once the seed of a new tune was planted in me it would germinate and grow, until I would find my whole being pulsating to its rhythm.

My father was a crack shot, both with rifle and shot-gun, and held international records in shooting duck and the Kashmiri partridge, the *chakor*. His shooting parties were meticulously planned, each guest provided with cartridges and a packed lunch complete with red wine. Duck shoots at Hokarsar and Higam, shallow lakes to the west of Srinagar, would begin early in the mornings. We would all drive out in a great procession, assemble on the banks of the lake, and at the appointed hour get into our boats and row to our respective 'butts'. There the whole day would be spent massacring duck of various species, including occasional wild geese. As a special treat my father would sometimes let me sit behind him while he was shooting, and I would click the gold counter whenever he dropped a bird. He would use three double-barrelled Webley & Scott shot-guns, with a loader standing behind him on either side. After firing the first gun he would hand it over to the man at his left and take a loaded one from the one on his right. By the time he had fired the next gun the previous one had been reloaded, and this relay would carry on for hours. I recall several occasions when a flight of duck came across the lake and my father dropped two birds with the first gun when the flight was just within range, another two with the second when it was overhead, and yet another two with the third when it had passed him but was still within range. I admired his skill tremendously.

At big game, also, he was superb. In the sub-valleys around Kashmir, and in the vicinity of Udhampur in the Jammu region, he had developed some excellent shooting reserves. I was with him on several occasions when he shot black bear, wild boar, panther and—alas—the magnificent Kashmir stag (the Hangul), which is now almost extinct. The air in the cold October mornings was crisp and clear, the hillsides ablaze in russet and gold, and the atavistic lure of the hunt caused the blood to flow faster through one's veins. Apart from shooting, the trout fishing in Kashmir is among the best in the world. A century ago my great-grandfather Maharaja Ranbir Singh had sent Queen Victoria a present of a pair of Kashmir pashmina goats. The man who came to get them reported back to Her Majesty that the mountain streams of Kashmir were ideally suited to trout, whereupon the redoubtable monarch sent back a return gift of a tank full of tiny trout fingerlings.

These flourished so well in Kashmir that they soon far outgrew their ancestors. In England a fish over a pound is considered a good catch; I have known days when my father would throw back anything under two. His largest catch was 14½ pounds, but in the Harwan hatchery a brown trout grew to an astonishing 27 pounds.

Accompanying my father on a fishing trip to Thricker and Nambal on the Liddar river coming down from Pahalgam was a cherished event. The stream flowed literally through the garden, and one would get up early and catch fish for breakfast. The whole day we would be out fishing, and in the evenings return to the lodge. If my father landed a good catch there was merriment; but if he had a bad day or lost a big fish he would be in a terrible mood. This almost invariably meant that some unfortunate servant or shikari was sacked in the middle of the night. All of us then sat quietly, listening to the sound of the petromax lamps and the stream flowing outside, not daring to speak.

In fact, father shared a trait common to the feudal order; he was a bad loser. Any small setback in shooting or fishing, polo or racing, would throw him into a dark mood which lasted for days. And this would inevitably lead to what came to be known as a 'muquaddama', a long inquiry into the alleged inefficiency or misbehaviour of some hapless young member of the staff or a servant. As I grew older these cruel inquisitions began to infuriate me and added to my growing alienation from the order into which I had been born. Here was authority without generosity; power without compassion.

Dachigam, just twelve miles from Srinagar, was one of my father's favourite haunts. Beyond the reservoir at Harwan where, twenty-four centuries ago, the second international Buddhist conclave is believed to have been held, the road turns into a steep valley. Four miles from the entrance to the reserve there is a clearing in which my father's famous shooting lodge was constructed. The game reserve teemed with black bear and wild boar, while in the autumn the magnificent Hangul would move down, along with the descending snowline. The lodge was simple but elegant, consisting of six bedrooms with attached baths, and a drawing and dining-room, the walls covered with beige silk. It commanded a spectacular view; heavily afforested mountains soared into the sky on three sides, while just behind the lodge a lower hill covered with grass and dotted with black boulders provided the perfect counterpoint. The garden had four large walnut trees, beds of multi-coloured roses, and lots of green lawn.

We came here at least half a dozen times in the season. My father would occasionally shoot a bear or pig—once he shot a bear from the veranda of the lodge—but more often there would just be a picnic. His shikari was a gnarled, sun-beaten Kashmiri called Rahman Wani, with a face like carved granite and impressive red moustaches. We came sometimes with my mother, her lady-in-waiting Wazirni Sita, and a wide assortment of relatives and maid servants, and played hide and seek in the compound among the rose bushes. The singing of the wind through the great trees, the softly insistent gushing of the stream that flowed through the valley, the blue of the sky and the green of the forest always in harmonious contrast, combined to give Dachigam a magical quality. One entered there an almost different dimension, a world where human beings were in a way redundant and the elements held their gracious sway over time and space.

Another marvellous spot was our cottage on an island in the Dal Lake which was originally my grandfather's pigeon house. This led it to be called 'Kotar Khana' in Kashmiri, and although it was subsequently renamed Lake Pavilion and then Lakshmi Kutir, the original name has stuck. The cottage commands a truly breathtaking view of the mountains spread out a hundred and eighty degrees like a gigantic amphitheatre. I have always loved being among mountains, though I have never been possessed of the desire to climb them. I like just looking at them, feeling them as exhilarating presences in my consciousness. Their poise, unhurried and imperturbable, provides a welcome contrast to the rush and bustle, the envy and intrigue, of daily life. I have had occasion to travel to the ends of the earth, and have found that all great mountain ranges— the Himalaya, the Alps, the Andes—share this very special quality of expanding human consciousness.

It was the stunning natural beauty of Kashmir that first taught me to ask deeper questions leading into the heart of the mystery that is life. In my early years my religious feelings were

2

largely confined to the traditional devotionalism of my mother
—genuine but somewhat limited. Looking back, though, it is
clear that the sheer physical beauty of Kashmir—its mountains
and valleys, rivers and forests, paddy fields and winding mountain tracks—helped to sharpen my awareness of beauty, to make
me more responsive to the softer and finer aspects of the human
spirit that are so often steam-rollered into the dust by the ham-
mering insistence of the life of the moment. Growing up in
beautiful natural surroundings is a rare and inestimable privilege. It is curious how in India we tend to ignore natural
beauty, so that children often remain quite unaware of this
dimension. In fact, it was my British guardians, and people like
Beryl Stileman, who constantly went into raptures over lovely
views and sunsets. At the time this rather amused us, and we
felt secretly superior on the assumption that India was evidently
much more beautiful than England. But gradually I began to
see our natural beauty with new, more open, eyes.

Social awareness does not come easily to a prince. I lived in
a self-contained world where servants were taken for granted
and the question of why some should be the rulers and others
the ruled was never formulated, far less asked. And yet I had
one advantage over others in my position. My mother was a
village girl from a poor family, and howsoever much she may
have liked the trappings and tinsel of royalty, she always considered it a sacred duty to alleviate the want and suffering of
the poor. Throughout her thirty years as Maharani she spent
large sums on helping not only poor relatives, but hundreds of
common folk in want and distress. It is impossible to recount
the number of girls she got married off, the houses for the poor
she had made, the clothes and sweets she would forever be
distributing. She always brought home to me the fact that I had
a duty to serve and help the poor. 'If you help the rich', she
would say, 'they will only take your money and turn upon you
when you stop giving. Help the poor, they will appreciate it
and pray for you and bless you.' In a way this was my introduc-
tion, if not to socialism, at least to the concept of distributive
justice. She would also enjoin upon me to acknowledge every
salutation with folded hands, to inquire after the welfare of
people's families, to mix with whosoever came, rich or poor.
'Your father never meets the people,' she would complain,

'that's the trouble. He just sits surrounded by fawning courtiers and favourites, and never really gets to know what is going on outside.'

Apart from a series of ADCs drawn from the Jammu and Kashmir State forces, both Hindu and Muslim, my father had a number of prominent Muslim courtiers. Chief among them was Nawab Khushru Jung, a nobleman from Hyderabad whose services had been loaned to my father by the Nizam. 'Mahboob' was a close friend as well as Military Secretary to my father for many years. He had an impressive presence with his rich voice and courtly manner, was an excellent horseman and also, as even we boys knew, a great ladies' man. Sahibzada Nur Mohammed Khan, a portly figure from Baluchistan, was on my father's staff for several years. Then there was Sardar Abdul Rahman Effendi—'Bhaijan'—who was a close friend of my father's and lived on Gupkar Road just outside our Srinagar palace gates. He was a refugee from Afghanistan, being related to King Amanullah who had been deposed and forced to flee the country. Effendi's second wife was a large woman with an amusing Pushto-Urdu accent; she played tennis with my mother, while Effendi's mother-in-law was a memorable personality known as Koko Jan. When I saw her she was almost eighty but still always the life of the party. Apparently she had played a prominent role in the Afghan court during her youth. There was never any differentiation between the Hindu and Muslim courtiers, and, if anything, the latter seemed to be more favourably treated. As far as office work was concerned, this was mainly managed by a diminutive but highly efficient Kashmiri Pandit, Dina Nath Jalali, who had been with my father for an incredible twenty-five years, and a taller associate, Shambhu Nath Wanchu.

Kashmir then, as now, was a tourist's delight, and a galaxy of Indian princes and other personages would come up every summer, some as guests of my father. I remember the strikingly beautiful Princess Niloufer, then unhappy in her marriage with the Nizam of Hyderabad's second son, and her less attractive cousin Princess Durisheshwar, wife of the Nizam's elder son the Prince of Berar. A whole spectrum of Maharajas, Rajas and Nawabs were around. Specially close was the Nawab of Palanpur and his beautiful Australian Begum. I would meet some of these princes and would have to touch their feet and call them 'Uncle'. On one such occasion I was fascinated to meet a man who was stone deaf, and with whom conversation had to be carried on by means of a writing tablet. He was the Maharaja of Jind, famous for his extensive kennel. It struck me even then that the money he lavished on his dogs could with greater advantage have been spent on the welfare of his people.

The British were much less in evidence. Unlike British India, where their presence was ubiquitous, in the Indian States they were generally not too visible. This was specially so in our State, because my father genuinely distrusted them and even persuaded them to move their residency in winter to Sialkot in the Panjab rather than to Jammu. For the summer months the British Resident lived on the bund in Srinagar in the house later converted into the Government Handicrafts Emporium, but we seldom saw him and I cannot remember a single occasion on which I met him at the Palace. He held a fancy dress party every year, however, which I would attend along with Digby and Bilti. The Resident's wife would call on my mother occasionally along with other foreign ladies and the wives of non-Kashmiri officials. Among these I recall Lady Dalal, wife of the Parsi Chief Justice, Sir Barjor Dalal, a gentle little woman who would give me tiny pencils whenever she came and which I collected avidly.

As for the Kashmiri Muslims, our contacts were mostly limited to the gardeners and the shooting and fishing guards. Once my father asked Ghulam Ahmed, a jeweller and carpet manufacturer of repute who was also his art adviser, to take me round the city. This he did, and I remember my astonishment at seeing all those dilapidated buildings on the Jhelum, looking as if they could topple any moment into the river. 'These are your people', Ahmed said somewhat dramatically. The visit had a rather disturbing effect upon me, and for days thereafter the recollection of the Jhelum dwellers would flash back upon me, their squalor in such glaring contrast to the orderly elegance of the palace as to constitute virtually a different world.

Of political developments in the State at the time, or the great freedom movement sweeping the nation, we knew little. The *Tribune* and the *Civil & Military Gazette*, both published from Lahore, came to the house, but I was not yet ten and was too young to be able to read or understand them. The haunting signature tune of All India Radio (happily unchanged to this day) is among my earlier recollections, and we occasionally listened in to the news, specially after the War had begun. But we had no real idea of what was happening, and lived in an isolated world far removed from the economic and political realities outside. Despite our comfortable surroundings, I can seldom recall being really happy as a child. There was somewhere deep within me a built-in fear, undefined but nevertheless clearly felt. Perhaps it was because of the unsatisfactory parental situation, or my enforced absence from my mother. Whatever it was, it vitiated a good deal of my early life.

I have mentioned how I was sent to Cathedral High School in Bombay in the winter of 1940 and 1941. In the summer of those years I started attending the Presentation Convent School in Raj Bagh, Srinagar. In order to avoid travelling through the city over Amira Kadal, the first of the seven historic bridges across the Jhelum, I had to drive to the river bank near Peston-jees and Ahdoos (shops that had virtually become institutions), cross the river in a *shikara* and alight on the opposite bank quite near the school. The car meanwhile was driven across the bridge and awaited me on the other side. Thinking back, it seems that, because the National Conference movement against Dogra rule led by Sheikh Abdullah had begun gaining momentum, my father thought it safer for me to avoid driving through the city, although this was never given as a reason. The Presentation Convent was clean and efficiently run by an estimable group of Irish nuns led by Mother Peter. Our class teacher was Sister Annunciata, while the genial head of the mission, Father Shanks, would visit the school from time to time. They were all Irish, and spoke with a distinctive accent. Apart from the studies at which (alas, I suspect, not entirely on merit) I invariably stood first, there were music and games and plays and many other pleasant activities. Lovely pictures of the Virgin Mary and Jesus hung on the walls, and the nuns were models of courteous and genuine solicitude. I remember my first appearance in a play—it was about Robin Hood, and we worked on it for days before the annual function when it was performed. I was first cast as King Richard, but at the last moment my role was changed to that of Robin Hood. I believe my father felt that, being a prince, I should not assume that I would always have to play the royal role.

My father, however, was modern only in some ways. I have mentioned that he and the then Maharaja of Jodhpur were for years close friends. Every year Umaid Singhji and his strong-willed wife would come up to Kashmir with their children—five boys and a girl called Susan. I suspect that there had been some talk of Susan and me getting engaged, because that is the only explanation for the peculiar events that followed. For some reason which I have never been able to discover, the friendship between the two Maharajas broke. My father, true to the feudal tradition, was an extremist in such matters. For him there was no area of grey; a person was either in or out. And so, as a sort of reaction just to spite the Jodhpurs, he rushed into getting me engaged to another Rathaur princess, the daughter of the then ruler of Ratlam, Maharaja Sajjan Singhji. It will leave modern readers aghast that there could be serious engagements at the age of ten plus, but this was in the early forties and in an Indian State, and the betrothal of the Yuvaraj was a great ceremonial event. There was a full-dress darbar in the lawns of Gulab Bhavan, described by Reuters as 'one of those splendid displays of colour and magnificence for which Darbars in India are famous'. I was dressed in brocade and jewels, and have a clear recollection of walking into the gathering feeling absolutely ridiculous. A Ratlam courtier, Vijay Bahadur, came at the head of their contingent. He dropped a sovereign just before he was to present it to me, and whispered to me to pretend to take one off his empty handkerchief so that no one would notice his lapse. This I solemnly did as he was a good sport and I did not want to let him down.

The Ratlam princess Chandra Kunwer, called 'Shanti', and her younger brother came up to Srinagar with their guardian, a Mrs Stewart, and spent some months there. She seemed very nice but I had not reached the age of taking an intelligent interest in girls. Some years later, when I was in America, we started corresponding with each other. But the situation was obviously absurd, and the irony of the charade was compounded when, as I will record later, my father in 1949 equally impulsively broke off the engagement. I had no say on either occasion, but it is clear that the matter was handled in a manner that can only be described as disgraceful, grossly unfair to the Ratlam family—and particularly Shanti—and did no credit to ours. I learnt that Shanti subsequently married someone in Uttar Pradesh and many years later was killed in an automobile crash.

Chapter 3

One of Colonel Haksar's grandsons, Vivek Nehru, was at the Doon School in Dehra Dun, which had been set up in 1935 on the pattern of the famous British public schools, the first of its kind in India. Colonel Haksar persuaded my father to send me there. Before this the Indian princes had either gone to school in England or to what were known as the 'princely' schools in Ajmer, Rajkot, Indore and other locations. Here the sons of the Indian aristocracy were educated, usually with the facility of private servants and lots of spending money. Sending me to the Doon School was, therefore, an imaginative and forward-looking decision which had a lasting influence upon my future life. Had I not been obliged to go through four rather unpleasant years at Doon, it would have been much more difficult for me to make the crucial transition from feudal to democratic life which lay only a few years ahead. At the time, however, the prospect was not a particularly appealing one. My mother wept copiously when I left, and ended fainting in the arms of her ladies-in-waiting. I was full of apprehension at the unknown life that awaited me at school where, as Colonel Haksar had repeatedly pointed out, I would have to make my own bed, polish my own shoes and be content with a pocket money of five rupees a month. Having spent my first eleven years in a sheltered and highly privileged situation, the change was obviously not going to be pleasant. Colonel Haksar himself escorted me to Dehra Dun, and in September 1942 I joined the school. I was allotted, expectedly, to Kashmir House and given the roll number 259.

My first few terms at school were miserable. I was desperately homesick, and wept as unobtrusively as I could every night before going to sleep. There were about a dozen rooms on each floor, four boys to a room, with two lavatories on each of the two floors of the house. I was never comfortable in the dark, and hated the damp bed sheets, the coarse blue blankets and the low slung mosquito nets. Luckily, I was never physically ill-treated by the other boys, but the fact that I was a prince was not something which particularly endeared me to them. A major difficulty arose because, largely due to the intensive coaching I was given in the months at home preceding my admission, I was placed two classes higher than usual for boys of my age. Although this was hailed by my parents as recognition of my outstanding intellectual capacities, it put me in a position where almost all the boys in my class were two years older than I, while those of my age were two classes below. In the result, I fitted in neither with my classmates nor with my age group. Added to this was the fact that I was rather timid and introverted, totally unprepared by my upbringing for the rough and tumble of public school life.

The food was virtually inedible, consisting largely of vegetables that I particularly loathed, such as turnips, cabbage and lady's fingers. The cumulative effect of all this, as can be imagined, was one of unrelieved distaste. The popular view that public schools are luxurious resorts for the pampered children of the affluent classes is entirely misconceived. Indeed, at least when I was there, the whole atmosphere was spartan and strict. Though I carefully refrained from giving any hint of this in my letters to my parents (files of the ones I wrote to my father came to me after his death), I vividly remember counting the days for term to end from the very first day, and also the feeling of hopeless resignation in the pit of my stomach every time I left home after the holidays.

The school routine was full, both with academic work as well as sports and hobbies. Although there was nothing extraordinary about the routine, I will describe it briefly because it contrasted sharply with my previous existence and involved considerable adjustment on my part. We had to get up at six to the sound of the huge gong rung by the resident chowkidar. Chota Hazri—a cup of milk and a slice of bread—would be followed by P.T. on the main field. While I somehow managed most of the drill, I was particularly mortified during the weekly visit to the gymnasium where, for some reason, I developed an irrational fear of doing a forward roll on the box. Whenever I mounted the box for the purpose I froze, and nothing would persuade me to do the somersault. Time and again I would find myself in the absurd situation of sitting on that confounded box with the whole class sniggering at my embarrassment. Even a talking to by the Headmaster, the formidable Mr A. E. Foot, did not have any effect, and throughout my school career I never managed to break that particular hoodoo. After P.T., which the whole school did together, the boys returned to their respective houses. There were four—Kashmir, Hyderabad, Jaipur and Tata—and it was in our houses that we spent most of the time. A wash, change, breakfast and then we were off to the school building for Assembly and classes where each teacher had an allotted room. After the morning classes we would return to our houses for lunch, some rest and then attend the afternoon classes. After tea there would be sports, in which every boy had to participate, then back to the houses for a bath, evening homework (for some strange reason known as 'toye-time'), dinner and then bed.

The academic standards at school were high, but I was always a reasonably quick learner and able to cope quite satisfactorily despite my age. There were as many as nine subjects for the Senior Cambridge, the examination for which the school prepared us. Teaching standards were generally satisfactory, but there were few teachers who left a permament impression on me. The most memorable was Mr V. S. Chari (later V. Siddarthachari of the Indian Foreign Service), who took us for English—my best subject—and was excellent. It was he who first introduced me to English poetry, and even if the class bell sounded to mark the end of his period, none of us moved a muscle until he had finished. The boys were not nearly as well-behaved with all the teachers, and this taught me the useful lesson that only by maintaining one's competence and dignity could one elicit the respect of others; being too lenient and indecisive was invariably exploited, specially by the bullies and roughnecks.

True to the public school obsession with physical fitness, there was a good deal of stress on excelling at games, team events as well as individual. The four houses competed fiercely against one another in every game, and the whole school took part in the annual Dehra Dun district sports meet. I was never in any of the school teams except chess, which I captained for two years. The sport I liked least was cross-country running, a dreadful ordeal in which we had to cover miles over the hillocks and ravines that surrounded the school, sides aching and lungs bursting. The school also provided a wide variety of hobbies from which we had to choose two. I chose music and carpentry, the latter because everyone else seemed to be doing it. Each boy had a Report Card which had to be filled in by his teachers every month. The system of punishments was interesting and unusual. Corporal punishment was forbidden, and the severest punishment (short of expulsion from school for really serious offences) was a Yellow Card. This involved an announcement on the school notice board, forgoing Tuck Shop (a much treasured privilege) for a month, no cinema (to which we were taken occasionally) for the next two occasions, and so on. A Red Card was for consistently bad performance in studies and also carried a set of liabilities, and a Blue Card could be given by house prefects for minor misdemeanours. I went through my entire school career with only one Yellow Card, which I got because the boy sitting next to me during a history test copied my faulty answer, as a result of which we both got caught.

In the middle of every term there was a three-day break during which we all went on various expeditions to the many attractive locations in which the Doon valley abounds—Doiwala, Lachiwala, Raiwala. The more adventurous older boys went off on climbing expeditions, but my own ventures were confined to rafting down the rivers nearby or simply hanging around the picnic site. I was a non-swimmer when I joined school, and it was some years before I overcame the fear of water and diving. In a public school timidity is not a particularly prized asset, and looking back it is clear to me that this deprived me of enjoying school as much as I might have. Unfortunately the original Kashmir housemaster, Jack Gibson, left for naval service the very term I joined, and returned only in my last term. The Headmaster, Mr Foot, was aloof and forbidding and in any case the school was structured in such a way as to make the house the real focus of a boy's life. In the result, while the age factor denied me the satisfaction of a large circle of friends, I also did not receive the benefit of contact with an outstanding housemaster. Added to this was the fact that my father had forbidden anyone to visit me while at school, and that there was no one with whom I could discuss my problems and uncertainties.

School did, however, have a silver lining in the shape of bi-annual vacations—two and a half months in summer and six

weeks in winter. After I joined Doon my separate establishment
at home was wound up, Digby and Bilti were sent back to their
homes, and I began spending the holidays with my parents.
These years, from 1943 to 1946, were the closest I got to a
normal family atmosphere in childhood, as they also happened
to coincide with a phase of comparative harmony between my
parents. The summer vacations were spent in Srinagar, where
we all lived in the main palace known as Gulab Bhavan, now
the Oberoi Palace Hotel. This handsome double-storey structure built on three sides of a rectangle commands a superb view
of the Dal Lake and reflected my father's keen architectural
interests. Unlike many contemporary princes, whose palaces
were vast Victorian monstrosities, our residence with its clean
lines and uncluttered exterior fitted in well with the mountains
that formed its backdrop. The forests came right down to the
back of the building; my father once shot a panther from the
main lawn, while the late Maharaja Sardul Singh of Bikaner
shot a bear from his bathroom window. ('One bare body against
another', as a friend remarked in later years.)

The front lawns were carefully manicured, and beds of
multi-coloured flowers shone brightly in the crisp Kashmir air,
distinctly crisper than it now is, many decades later. The palace
was tastefully furnished, with exquisite European and Chinese
curios, and wall-to-wall carpeting in every room and corridor.
A lot of furniture came periodically from England through a
Mrs Sutherland, the widow of an Englishman who had been
Inspector-General of Police in the State at the crucial juncture
around the time of my birth, when the Muslim Conference
under Sheikh Abdullah first launched its anti-Dogra movement.
Apart from the carpets, which were made in Kashmir, all the
other furnishings, fabrics and fittings were European. My
parents occupied inter-connecting wings on the first floor of
the southern block, while I had a lovely suite on the ground
floor directly overlooking the lake. It was only after being exposed to the grim surroundings of the Doon School that I began
to appreciate the quiet elegance and beauty of our houses which
I had thus far taken for granted.

It now became evident that my father also looked forward to
my vacations. We would go out on fishing trips and to Dachigam for shooting-cum-picnics, and played lots of rummy, back-

gammon and ludo sitting out in the front lawn under one of the Chinar trees. Victor Rosenthal and the Stilemans were usually up in Srinagar at the time, which added to our fun. We spent hours working out lists for lunch and dinner parties, seating plans and menus. Both my parents were excellent cooks, and at least once a week there would be a cooking party. We all sat out in the lawn or the black marble porch in the centre of the main block, and then the cooking would begin. Liveried servants with yellow turbans brought in low asbestos stands about six inches high and five by three feet in area. On these would be placed coal stoves, and on them silver *patilas*, deep cooking dishes of various sizes depending on the item to be prepared. All the ingredients, carefully weighed and neatly arranged, were brought on folding tables. Three or four people cooked, including my parents, while the others watched and chatted. The chief taster was Wazir Tej Ram, a seasoned courtier a few years older than my father who, along with Faqir Singh, was a regular dinner guest at the palace.

Whisky would be served in small glasses, but I seldom saw my father taking more than his standard quota of three double pegs. This was when he would loosen up a bit and relax, and unless some staff problem erupted the atmosphere was comparatively free of tension. The cooking-cum-drinking-cum-gossip parties would last for several hours, dinner not being served till around eleven. I would sit in for the first couple of hours, then my dinner was brought on a tray at nine and I would eat while the rest kept up the party. After dinner I was allowed to stay on for a few minutes, and then at nine-thirty I withdrew, taking leave of my parents by touching their feet and bowing to the rest of the company. I would go off to my room and fall contentedly asleep with the sound of the party wafting faintly across the lawn.

I did not have any friends of my own age, but cousins from my mother's side were allowed to come and play with me from time to time. I met the girls at my mother's apartments, while the boys came to my room or we would play in the garden. The oldest boy, Nasib Chand, a few years older than I, was my favourite and the closest I had to a real friend.

During the summer holidays there were occasional official functions, which my father detested. He was a strange person;

highly intelligent and talented in many ways, but shy and uneasy in public. In fact he often said to his friends that he was only waiting for me to be twenty-one so that he could hand over the State responsibilities and then do the things he loved— shoot, fish, cook, race and build. It is a strange irony that twenty-one was in fact the age at which I took over from him what remained of his authority, but under circumstances that could not have been even remotely imagined at the time.

My father started training me early for public life. My first public speech was at the age of eleven, when I opened the annual exhibition at Srinagar, a combination of a trade and industries fair, entertainment complex and general fiesta, which had become an annual event. The opening took place during my summer vacation, so it became a regular fixture for me to perform the inauguration. I recall vividly reading out my first speech, heart quaking inwardly but managing somehow to display a blasé exterior. After the speech Colonel Haksar took me to Dachigam where my father awaited me with obvious pride. He was not a demonstrative person, but it was not difficult to gauge his feelings at any given moment. Some years later, in 1945, Gopalaswami Ayyangar recalled this incident when he wrote in a letter to my mother: 'Tiger must be quite a young man now. . . . I well remember the first public speech he made when I was in the State and how greatly it was appreciated for the correct enunciation and self-confidence with which he delivered it to a large audience.'

While the summer vacations were spent in Srinagar, the winter holidays were in Bombay, where my parents would go for several months of the year. In Bombay our whole life revolved around racing. My father was for years a leading patron of the turf, and maintained a string of superb race horses. These were stabled in the Mahalakshmi area near the racecourse, and every evening my father went to the stables and watched his horses go round and round the enclosure. There were gallops and spurts, small race books and large ones, confabulations with jockeys and trainers, thinly veiled animosity towards rival owners and, finally, race day on Saturday or Sunday. It seemed as if the whole week was a preparation for this event. My father invariably had at least two horses running, often as many as four. His scarlet and gold colours were familiar to every

Bombay race-goer, and for many years he was the leading owner, bagging many of the most prestigious races. He was a fine judge of horse flesh, and took great pains to select youngsters at the annual bloodstock sales in Bombay. As a logical culmination of this he started a stud farm of his own at Nagbani, a few miles outside Jammu, where by the time he died he had assembled some of the best stallions and brood mares in the country. Quite clearly, my father was much happier racing than administering the State, which chore he left largely to his carefully chosen Prime Minister and a small Council of Ministers, mostly from outside Jammu and Kashmir. In fact, although he enjoyed absolute power, he conducted himself rather like a constitutional monarch and hardly ever interfered with the administration of his Council of Ministers. In this regard he was far in advance of most of his princely contemporaries in India.

For me the holidays were an eagerly awaited event. They flashed by much too fast, unlike terms at school which seemed unending. Quite apart from superspace and time-warps, I learnt early that time does not flow at a uniform rate, at least for a homesick schoolboy. In due course I gradually began to get more adjusted to school life, though I did not make many abiding friendships. In fact, I generally disliked being at school, but I can see quite clearly that, had I remained at home or gone to one of the feudal establishments, I would probably have been hopelessly spoilt and quite unfit to meet the challenges that—unknown to me—lay only a few years ahead.

My only regret is that because of my father's strictness and the absence of an outstanding housemaster, I did not have any strong figure upon whom I could rely during those formative years, someone who might have filled the inner vacuum of uneasy insecurity that afflicted me. I remember once how a casual remark by Pandit Ramchandra Kak (appointed my guardian after Colonel Haksar) to the effect that he had great hopes and faith in my future as Yuvaraj gave me tremendous sustenance for months. Pandit Kak was in many ways a remarkable man, arrogant but unflinching in his adherence to the principles in which he believed. He would tell me that the greatest quality one could develop was 'poise', a calm imperturbability in the face of any circumstance, howsoever unsettling, and he displayed this himself in the adversity that he faced only a few years later.

Meanwhile, I had entered my teens, and the eternal mystery of the human body had begun to unfold itself as it has done for aeons, the same yet ever new. Those are breathtaking years for a boy, the first, tentative probings into manhood, the stunning discovery of hitherto unimagined dimensions of the human body. Kashmir is a marvellous place for such an awakening; the air crisp and cool, the doves cooing melodiously in the distance, the great Chinars rearing their heads high against a powder blue sky, and a boy on the threshold of manhood—bewildered, awestruck, ecstatic.

I had developed the habit of reading when I was quite small, and by the time I was finishing school I was a prolific reader. My favourites at that time were the thrilling Scarlet Pimpernel novels of Baroness Orczy and the hilarious Jeeves stories of P. G. Wodehouse. This apart, there were Dickens, Scott, Hardy and other British classics; Maupassant, Dumas and Victor Hugo among the French; Tolstoy, Chekhov and Gorki among the Russians. Poetry I always loved, and at one stage knew dozens of poems from *Palgrave's Golden Treasury* by heart. I discovered soon that I had a sharper memory than most other boys, specially when it came to verse. I think this was due to the rhythmic aspects of poetry, so closely allied to music. I was also interested in acting, and took a fairly active part in house and school plays. My high point was portraying Olivia in *Twelfth Night*, happily well before my voice cracked, and later I began directing plays with smaller boys in them.

Films were also an important element in my life at that stage. Apart from oriental fantasies with John Hal, Maria Montez and Sabu, there were remarkable Indian films like *Bharat Milap* and *Ram Rajya*, Vijay Bhat's famous historical films which brought the Ramayana to life for a whole generation; *Sikander*, with Sohrab Modi and Prithviraj; *Pukar*, with Naseem and Sohrab Modi; *Shakuntala* with Jayshree and Chandramohan; *Rajputani* with Bipin Gupta's splendid portrayal of Rana Pratap; *Chandragupta* with Nayampalli as an unforgettable Chanakya, and many others. The abiding impact of films on impressionable young minds is often underestimated by adults, with malign results that now speak for themselves.

Despite a few bad patches I was able to do well in my studies, and as the major examination neared I got better and more self-confident. I sat for the Senior Cambridge examination in December 1945, the year the Second World War ended. The centre was in our own school, but there were invigilators from outside. The papers in those days were set in England and corrected there, with the exception of Hindi. By this time I had outgrown many of my early inhibitions, and was for the first time actually beginning to enjoy being at school. There was a further examination offered by the Doon School at that time, the Intermediate Examination of the U.P. Board of Education. This was divided into Inter-Science and Inter-Arts, and almost invariably the brighter boys chose Science. I was quite clear, however, that for the public life to which I appeared destined Arts, which included economics, civics and history, would be more suitable. When I returned for the first term of 1946 after the Senior Cambridge, therefore, I joined Inter-Arts and found myself at one stroke head and shoulders above the rest of the class, all the brighter boys having predictably chosen Science. The Senior Cambridge results were announced during the term, and I secured a first division. I sent a telegram—my first —home, and was soon inundated by congratulatory telegrams not only from my father but from many of his loyal subjects. The school office had never before received so many telegrams, and this caused quite a flutter. I must admit that I was rather pleased with myself, particularly as I had been able to overcome the two-year age barrier and do better than many older boys in my class.

It was a measure of the isolation of our school from the winds of change blowing across the subcontinent that almost till our last year we were barely aware of the political developments that were gathering momentum and would within a year create an India free but divided. Although we read first about the Cripps Mission and then the Cabinet Mission led by a worthy gentleman whom we revelled in calling Lord 'Pathetic' Lawrence, we did not have any real awareness of the tremendous forces that were at work to create a new era in modern history. Our sympathies were, naturally, with Gandhiji, but the

3

boys at school were mainly children of Indian Civil Servants, Service Officers and rich businessmen, who could hardly be expected to be in the mainstream of the national movement.

At just about this time, I came across Jawaharlal Nehru's *Autobiography*. I was enthralled. Here was an intelligent and sensitive man, born to comfort but aligning himself fully with the hopes and aspirations of millions. Reading that book at that particular moment was a revelation. It brought home to me for the first time some awareness of the power of historical forces, of the inevitability of change, of the grandeur of a national liberation movement. I followed this up rapidly with his *Discovery of India*, which opened up for me a new world of the mind. I had, of course, a generalized pride in being Indian, but never before had the long and rich panorama of our history unrolled before me, nor had I appreciated the rich diversity and almost miraculous unity that had characterized India from the very dawn of human history. Reading Jawaharlal's two books gave me a new awareness, and strengthened the aversion to feudalism that had already been growing within me. I realized clearly that the old feudal structure was on the verge of collapse, and that, in any case, my father's life was not for me. What the alternative was I did not know, but inwardly I was ready for change.

Chapter 4

The storm in fact was almost ready to break. Centuries of Western colonialism were on the verge of ending, and the movement towards freedom of hitherto subject peoples—the greatest of its kind in the long panorama of human history—was nearing a triumphant conclusion with India in the vanguard. Something deep was stirring in our vast and ancient land. India was rising again, the miracle of renewal was once again ready to occur. The most destructive war ever fought by mankind had just ended. My father had gone to England in the course of the war as a member of Winston Churchill's War Cabinet, evidently one of those elaborate farces at which the imperial British excelled, aimed at giving members of the British Empire some sort of symbolic say in the affairs of State without any real power to influence decisions. He was in London for some of the worst German bombing, and on his return related to us how, despite the air raid sirens, not a single person would leave his theatre seat for the shelters. Earlier he had paid a visit to the State Forces in the Middle East, and on his return had been given a rousing reception by the people.

My mother, also, was very active during the war days. She organized a War Aid Committee and she and the leading ladies of Srinagar would meet regularly to knit, sew and prepare pickles for troops in the forward areas. Indeed she did so well that she was awarded 'The Crown of India', a decoration reserved for distinguished women and received earlier only by two or three other Indians. She was, of course, thrilled with the whole affair, specially so as in the same year's imperial honours list my father received a decoration that was slightly lower in the hierarchy of protocol. She was also very advanced in some of her views regarding social customs. In 1947 she created history by including Harijan girls, generally regarded at that time as untouchable, among the nine who are worshipped during the sacred *Navratras*.

My first term in the Intermediate class, which I enjoyed more than any earlier one, was marred only by an unexpected development that was to have a great effect on my life. I gradually began developing a sharp, biting pain in my right hip whenever my leg would fall outwards in sleep. I never discovered what caused this, perhaps some trauma during all those riding falls I had earlier, but as the frequency of the pain increased I began to feel more and more alarmed. I did not tell anyone about it for months, a mistake understandable enough for a boy of fifteen, but one that cost me a stiff hip for the rest of my life.

The term ended and we left for our respective homes, fully expecting to return when the next term was due. However, by mid-1946 the communal situation in India had greatly deteriorated. Hindu–Muslim riots broke out with increasing frequency and ferocity, and with the stage set for the British withdrawal the Congress and the Muslim League were locked in deadly combat. Some vague threats about the possibility of my being kidnapped or harmed in some way at school had begun to circulate during that last term, but, of course, we pooh-poohed the whole matter. None the less, my father—aided and abetted no doubt by my mother—decided that it was too risky to send their only son and heir to a far-away school when the country was on the verge of a major cataclysm. Perhaps they were right, but when I learnt of the decision soon after I came to Srinagar for the summer vacation I was very upset. It was, I thought, strange irony that in the years when I detested going to school I was ruthlessly packed off to it, and just when I was beginning to enjoy it was peremptorily withdrawn.

However, as usual, I had little say in the matter, and when my mother ecstatically broke the news to me I didn't have the heart to make a scene. Thus ended my four years at the Doon School, years of painful adjustment and unappetizing food, but also of valuable training in self-reliance which stood me in good stead for the rest of my life. I am not overly sentimental about the old school tie, but I do acknowledge a debt of gratitude to my father for having sent me to the Doon, and to the school itself for having, in its own rather rough way, saved me from growing up in a feudal environment and given me a useful intellectual grounding.

Although my stay at the Doon had been disrupted, I was keen to continue my studies and persuaded my father to send me to the local Sri Pratap College in Srinagar. This he agreed to do, an event which at the time was regarded as a progressive and democratic gesture. I went to college every day accompanied by an ADC, but sat in the classroom with the other students. I took English, civics, history and economics, and also participated in debates and declamation contests. On one occasion I won a declamation prize, which was presented by my mother at the annual prize-giving. Unfortunately, my stay at college turned out to be very short, confined only to the summer of 1946. My tutor at that time was Professor B. K. Madan, a genial and shrewd Kashmiri Pandit who, though no genius, was generally alert and well informed. His main lesson to me, quite in keeping with his character, was that packaging was more important than content. 'Tissue paper and tin foil', he would say, 'is all that really matters; it is *how* a thing is presented that really impresses most people, only few care to find out *what* in fact it really contains.' Cynical doctrine, no doubt, but not devoid of usefulness in this imperfect world.

Meanwhile, a strange development took place in our household. A certain Swami Sant Dev, who had lived in the State decades earlier in the time of the late ruler, Maharaja Pratap Singh, and was reported to have been banished by my father when he ascended the throne, staged a mysterious comeback. He came on to the scene around 1944, and by 1946 had firmly ensconced himself as Rajguru and was installed by my father in the beautiful Chashmashahi Guest House in Srinagar and the house where I lived as a child in Jammu. My father was far from being a religious man, but to everyone's amazement he suddenly became a devout disciple of Swamiji, sitting for long periods on the ground before him and never smoking in his presence. Swamiji was presented by him with lovely silk robes, a silver hookah and many other amenities, including a car. He was a remarkable man in many ways, erudite in several fields of knowledge and pink-complexioned even in his advanced age. He would never actually reveal how old he was, but it was rumoured that he was well over eighty (some claimed a hundred). He took opium regularly and would often nod off to sleep, a phenomenon interpreted by his followers as proof of his direct contact with God.

Much maligned though he subsequently was, I feel that his influence on my father's personal life was all to the good. He urged him to cut down on his smoking and drinking, and generally tempered his rather aggressive nature with some sort of religious commitment, howsoever superficial. Also, he was an influence in bringing my parents closer to each other. My mother being deeply religious was, of course, delighted at this turn of events, and her elder brother, Thakur Nachint Chand— who was for many years the Deorhi Officer or Chamberlain— grew in importance at the court as an intermediary between Swamiji and my father. I also had to see Swamiji regularly, but what with my hip pain was beginning to find it increasingly difficult to sit crosslegged on the floor, and so rather avoided going there. Swamiji always treated me with great affection. He was a connoisseur of classical music, and enjoyed hearing me sing his favourite raga, Jaijaiwanti.

It was in the political sphere that Swamiji's influence proved to be disastrous. As with many of the larger Indian States, the prospect of becoming an independent ruler after the British withdrawal was an alluring one for my father. He had never taken happily to British suzerainty, and at the same time was far too deeply enmeshed in the feudal tradition to really come to terms with the democratic forces that were gaining momentum in the subcontinent and within the State itself. A major weakness of the feudal system is that the rulers are told only what their courtiers think they want to hear, which is seldom in consonance with what is in fact happening. It was on this feudal ambition that Swamiji astutely played, planting in my father's mind visions of an extended kingdom sweeping down to Lahore itself, where our ancestor Maharaja Gulab Singh and his brothers Raja Dhyan Singh and Raja Suchet Singh had played such a crucial role a century earlier. There is also some reason to believe that Swamiji was in touch with some of the Congress leaders, and that Acharya Kripalani's visit to the State early in 1947 was a direct result of his intervention.

Be that as it may, the end of Dogra rule was fast approaching, although my father seemed to be blissfully unaware of the tremendous forces that were on the move in the subcontinent. Within the State Sheikh Abdullah had converted his Muslim Conference, founded in 1931, to the National Conference and had developed personal and ideological links with Jawaharlal Nehru. He was active in the State's people's movement which was a sort of counterpart in the Indian States of the wider anti-British movement of the Indian National Congress. Although Abdullah was never really trusted by the more conservative Congress leaders like Sardar Patel, he succeeded in gaining the close confidence of Jawaharlal who, perhaps because of his Kashmiri origin, looked upon Kashmir as his special sphere of interest.

Jinnah had little use for Abdullah and his associates, partly because the Sheikh was not prepared to toe his line and partly because of Jinnah's messianic belief that he and his Muslim League were the sole guardians of Muslim interests in the sub-continent. Abdullah's tactics were simple but effective. Surcharged as he always was with anti-Dogra feelings, he played skilfully on Nehru's anti-feudalism by making my father the main target of his political assault. In May 1946 Sheikh Abdullah and his National Conference launched a 'Quit Kashmir' agitation on the lines of Gandhiji's celebrated 'Quit India' movement four years earlier. Prior to that my father had taken some steps towards popular government in the State, including a dyarchy experiment in 1944 with the setting up of a partially elected Praja Sabha. But this did not satisfy the National Conference's demand for a full share in State power. In 1945 the Sopore session of that party had been attended by Jawaharlal Nehru and Khan Abdul Ghaffar Khan, and the Indian National Congress, which was generally backing the State People's Conference, had shown special interest in Kashmir in view of the impending partition and the close personal friendship between Jawaharlal Nehru and Sheikh Abdullah. Unfortunately, my father was not able to grasp the historic dimensions of the changes that were around the corner. This is amply borne out by the fact that when on 20 May Sheikh Abdullah and a number of other National Conference workers were arrested, and Jawaharlal Nehru announced his intention to visit the State, his entry was banned. Characteristically, Jawaharlal decided to defy the ban and enter Kashmir from the Panjab via the Kohala bridge. A company of State Forces troops commanded by a Gurkha officer, Major Bhagwan Singh, stood with bayonets fixed half-way across the bridge. Jawaharlal, fearless as ever, walked across and pushed the bayonets aside. By a stroke of good fortune Bhagwan Singh was a tactful and intelligent man. He ordered his troops aside, politely asked Jawaharlal to come across the bridge and informed him that he was under arrest.

The news reached us in Gulab Bhavan, and Pandit Kak, the then Prime Minister, reported to my father with subdued pride and excitement that Jawaharlal had been arrested. I was stunned. Here was the most charismatic leader of the national movement for freedom, the author of the *Autobiography* and *Discovery of India*, the declared future Prime Minister of the Indian Republic, and, instead of welcoming him and seeking his co-operation, we had arrested him. I have no doubt that his arrest was the turning point in the history of the State. Jawaharlal was brought to Srinagar, and after three days the Congress Working Committee persuaded him to come back to India. Later in July the State Government lifted the ban on his entry and he did come and interview Sheikh Abdullah in jail. But it was too late; the die had been cast, and it was only a matter of time before disaster struck.

It has always seemed to me tragic that a man as intelligent as my father, and in many ways as constitutional and progressive, should have in those last years so grievously misjudged the political situation in the country. He was generally an enlightened ruler, having, for example, thrown all temples in the State open to Harijans as far back as 1932. On that occasion the Raj Pandit in Jammu, who was head priest of our family temple the Sri Raghunath Mandir, had opposed the move. My father dismissed him peremptorily, and appointed his brother in his place only after he had unequivocally agreed to accept the Harijans. Similarly, in many matters relating to land tenure and administration my father had introduced reforms far in advance of most other Indian States. Having appointed his Ministers, the Muslim contingent usually from U.P., he would not interfere with their working. Indeed, there was a case when a citizen of Jammu living just outside our palace challenged in court my father's decision to acquire his property, and successfully prevented the move. In fact when at the age of thirty he ascended the throne on 23 September 1925 he had proclaimed 'Justice is my religion and merit alone will be considered the deciding factor for all types of employment. Caste, creed, religion or sex will receive no consideration.' During his reign he introduced a number of administrative and political reforms, culminating in 1944 in an experiment in dyarchy. Under this the Praja Sabha, set up a decade earlier, was given the right to nominate a panel of six, out of which he would choose two persons to join the Council of Ministers. This, for the first time, introduced a 'popular' element in the government, and towards the end of 1944 two such Ministers were appointed, Mirza Afjal Beg and Wazir Ganga Ram, who had secured the highest votes among the Muslim and Hindu candidates respectively.

Again, unlike most other rulers, my father made a clear distinction between his private property, including jewellery, and State property. He left family jewellery, shawls, carpets and regalia worth crores with the State *Toshakhana* (Treasury), which most others in his place would have appropriated without turning a hair. He never harassed the population for personal ends, living an aloof and self-contained life in the palace. His administration and system of justice is to this day accepted by impartial observers as having been much fairer than those of the post-1947 period. Corruption was far less, and severely punished whenever it came to light.

Being a progressive ruler was one thing; coping with a once-in-a-millennium historical phenomenon was another. There were four major forces at work on the subcontinent at that time, and my father was on hostile terms with each one of them. There were the British, ready at last to surrender the brightest jewel in their Empire. Although he never really believed until the very end that they would actually go, my father was too much of a patriot to strike any sort of surreptitious deal with them. There was the Indian National Congress, inspired by Gandhiji and led by Jawaharlal, Vallabhbhai Patel, Maulana Azad and other giants of the freedom movement. To this party my father was hostile mainly because of Jawaharlal's close association with his arch enemy Sheikh Abdullah. Then there was the Muslim League led by Mohammad Ali Jinnah. Although this party supported the right of rulers to decide the fate of their respective States, and in Kashmir opposed Sheikh Abdullah and his National Conference tooth and nail, my father was enough of a Hindu not to be able to stomach the aggressive Muslim communalism of the League, and this led him to spurn tempting offers from Pakistan. Finally, there was the main political party in the State itself, the National Conference led by Sheikh Abdullah, with whom my father was at loggerheads for decades because he looked upon it as the major threat to his throne and Dogra rule. The net result was that, when the crucial moment came, all the forces that counted were arrayed on the opposite side of the fence. Added to this was my father's disinclination to take a firm decision one way or the other. Thus he found himself alone and friendless, and the edifice of Dogra power built up so painstakingly over a century collapsed. If only I had been ten years older, I felt, I could have changed history. But if I *had* been ten years older, might I also not have fallen victim to the feudal virus?

Despite the excitement caused by the arrest of Nehru, things seemed to settle down again for a while. I spent that summer going to college in Srinagar and, on weekends, accompanying my parents on shooting and fishing expeditions. I was allowed for the first time to try my hand at big game. My father gave me a .318 rifle, and for my first major shoot I was sent to Dachigam with Thakur Harnam Singh Pathania, a crack shot who was a senior officer in our forest service and later rose to be Chief Conservator. We set out early in the morning, and entered the reserve before sunrise. The cold air was fragrant with the aroma of the forest, and the mountains seemed alive and vibrant in that early dawn. I can still savour the sense of exhilaration that I felt as, gun in hand, we made our way through the forest. The sun came up after a while, setting the forests on the surrounding mountain slopes ablaze in their autumn colours. Our quarry was the magnificent Kashmir stag, but we did not come across one. A few doe, their eyes gentle and liquid, stood frozen until we approached quite near and then bolted off into the forest.

At around ten, after we had driven in the reserve a good deal, Harnam Singh suddenly caught my hand and whispered, 'Would you like to have a shot at a bhaloo?' About a hundred yards away, partially obscured by some trees, stood a huge black bear. I raised my rifle and fired. The bullet knocked the bear clean over, but they are tough creatures and, unless

mortally wounded, are difficult to recover. Cautiously we
moved towards the spot where the bear had fallen, Harnam
Singh keeping his rifle at the ready. We found blood but no
trace of the bear. It is said that bears have secret hideouts where
they go when ill or wounded, and that they can treat their
wounds with healing herbs from the forests. Be that as it may,
we never found the bear. Perhaps it was symbolic; I was not
destined to be a hunter, and some years later I gave up shooting
and fishing for good.

The summer rounded off into the superb Kashmir autumn;
the Chinar leaves began to turn russet, the paddy ripened and
its golden fields shone against the green of the valley. The air
was crisp with expectation. Great things were happening on
the subcontinent; the Cabinet mission came and went, Jinnah's
demand for a divided India shook the subcontinent to its
foundations. Lord Wavell, the square, one-eyed Viceroy was
replaced by the dashing and handsome Lord Mountbatten and
his beautiful wife Edwina. History was in the wings waiting to
make a dramatic appearance. And yet we were almost entirely
bogged down in petty affairs—the ridiculous little intrigues at
my father's court, the circle of small-minded men surrounding
him, the coterie of time-servers and yes-men hanging around
interminably.

Swamiji's influence continued to grow, and with it the rise to
power in court of my mother's elder brother Thakur Nachint
Chand. He had been a non-commissioned officer in the Dogra
regiment when my mother's marriage took place and, as was
customary, had been given a large jagir and made a ranking
courtier after the event. He was for many years the Chamberlain to my mother, over whom he wielded great influence, being
many years older and having once, when she was a child, saved
her from drowning in the village pool at Bijeypur. While he was
a shrewd and basically loyal person, his intellectual horizons
were limited and he was greatly given to seeking the magic
favours of Swamis and Sadhus. There was no doubt that in the
very difficult years that my mother spent after her marriage,
a village girl suddenly transported into the vortex of court
intrigue, he was a tower of strength to her, and he seldom lost
an opportunity of pointing out how, had it not been for him,
she would have fallen victim and perished long before I was

born. In this he incurred the displeasure of the opposing faction at court, and was generally unpopular and disliked by the Jamwal baradari, my father's kinsmen. With the advent of Swamiji, however, he suddenly rose to prominence and became the main courier between him and my father.

We moved down to Jammu for the season as usual in the first week of November. My tutor Professor Madan had made inquiries and found that I could take the Intermediate examination of Allahabad University as a private student. My father was not very keen on the idea, he himself never having gone beyond Matriculation at Mayo College, but Madan and my mother succeeded in persuading him to agree. For this I owe a deep debt of gratitude to Madan Sahib, for if my studies had broken off at that point it would have been impossible for me to take them up again as I did later. A special examination centre was opened in one of our Jammu staff houses, and early in 1947 I appeared for the examination taking English, civics, economics and Hindi. Considering the fact that after the Senior Cambridge my studies had consisted of a term at the Doon, a term at Srinagar College and a few months of rather hurried private coaching at Jammu, I was quite pleased to get through the examination in the second division.

I was growing up rapidly and, looking back, I can see that the corrosive influence of a feudal court had begun insidiously to influence my behaviour. I began to get overbearing in my attitude to the servants, to treat the dogs roughly and generally to start developing those traits that constitute the less desirable features of feudal life. Being deprived of virtually any company of my age—Nasib was away in college at Lucknow—I spent more and more time with the staff. My mother and father seemed to be coming somewhat closer, though the basic tension remained, often bursting out into searing scenes which left me deeply mortified. My mother at this time lived in Amar Mahal, the large brick chateau that my grandfather had started building in Jammu but never completed, while my father lived in the low, grey house next to it known as Hari Niwas, where I also had a room. My mother would come across for meals, and we would all play a good deal of rummy and backgammon. Our life in Jammu was even more isolated than in Srinagar. The only place we visited was Udhampur, a town forty miles from

Jammu, where my father had developed some fine shooting reserves. He also built a residence there named—to my pleasure and surprise—Tara Niwas, after my mother. There we would all stay before going out to the various *rakhs* for shoots. Though lacking the magnificence of the Kashmir mountains, the hills around Udhampur nurtured a wide variety of large and small game including panther and wild boar.

All these months the pain in my right hip joint had continued to increase steadily. I began to dread falling asleep at night because of the sharp, shooting pain that would occur. The muscles of my right hip and leg began to atrophy, as a result of which I began limping slightly. Whenever my mother remarked on this I would brush the matter aside, but one day my father noticed it also and asked the Palace physician, Dr S. K. Shangloo, to examine me. It was then that he discovered the muscle atrophy. He started me on some oil massage for a few weeks, but it made no difference. Ultimately my father decided that I should go to Bombay for specialist consultation. The Controller Household, Brigadier N. S. Rawat, accompanied me and I went through a series of tests and X-rays, including a visit to the famous Dr Khanolkar, founder of the Tata Cancer Institute. Evidently someone had suspected cancer, but this was ruled out. We were advised that if the pain did not disappear within three months it would be necessary to put me into a plaster cast to immobilize the joint for a while.

With this depressing news I returned to Jammu. My father, as usual, spent most of his time from March onwards in the swimming pool where, in the evenings, he played water polo with the staff and selected servants. I was not much of a swimmer, and took only a perfunctory part in the proceedings. I would wander off to Amar Mahal to spend some time with my mother, or down to Karan Niwas where Swamiji lived. In fact, I was at a loose end, and deeply disturbed by the hip pain and the general atmosphere. The summer grew upon us, but my father showed little inclination to fix a date for the move to Srinagar. Ultimately, my mother intervened, saying that it was getting intolerably hot in Jammu. This led to a strangely sharp reaction from my father, who took the suggestion with very ill grace and sulked about it for days. Looking back, I wonder whether he had some sort of premonition that this was to be his last visit to Kashmir as ruler.

We finally got up to Srinagar towards the end of May, and immediately plunged into hectic activity in connection with the forthcoming visit of the new Viceroy, Lord Louis Mountbatten, and Lady Mountbatten. Viceregal visits to Indian States were a regular feature of British rule, and I vaguely remember Lord Linlithgow having come sometime in the thirties when I was a small boy and presenting me with a gold-ringed riding stick. But this visit was special, not only because the British had already announced that they would leave India soon and hand over power but also, at least as far as I was concerned, because of the personalities involved. Coming as they did soon after the rather dour and unprepossessing Lord Wavell, the glamorous Mountbattens were an exciting contrast and I was eager to meet them.

My father was meticulous in making ceremonial arrangements; programmes were neatly printed and bound in golden paper with a maroon bow (gold and maroon being the State colours), and all details including guest lists and menus worked out down to the last detail. He would spend hours over such details, and the whole household was in a permanent state of tension, for if anything went wrong someone's head was sure to roll. As I was doing nothing particular at the time I also took a hand in helping out with staff duties, although my contribution was, to say the least, marginal. The great day finally came, and the Viceroy and Vicereine arrived to the booming of guns (I can't remember how many, but as my father himself ranked a 21-gun salute I presume the Viceroy got 31). I was at the porch with my mother and father to greet them. My first look confirmed and fulfilled all my expectations. They were every inch a charmed couple, and at once—and irrevocably—I associated them with my favourite characters from the Baroness Orczy novels, Sir Percy Blakeney and his beautiful wife Marguerite. They looked as if they had stepped out of the pages of one of these novels; he tall, handsome, dashing; she beautiful, gracious, charming. My boyish imagination, long in search of a break from the rigid atmosphere of our own court, found in the Mountbattens a marvellous window where fact and fantasy mingled.

Despite their aristocratic background, there was nothing

stuffy or formal about them and I was delighted at their informality and sense of humour. My father had introduced me as 'Tiger' and they called me that throughout the visit and, in fact, ever after. There was a whole series of garden parties and banquets and receptions. Two amusing incidents stand out. At the banquet there was a bell under the table, which my father was supposed to press when the party was over and the band was to play 'God save the King'. Mountbatten, sitting next to him, was tall and his knee hit against the bell by mistake in the course of the dinner, at which point the band dutifully struck up the anthem and all of us struggled gamely to our feet roughly half-way through the chicken curry. My father was furious and went red in the face, but luckily there was no one he could blame. Mountbatten laughed uproariously when he discovered what had happened, and a fit of giggles had me almost rolling on the floor despite my mother's glares from across the table. The second incident was when my father had to introduce his senior officials to the Viceroy before a garden party. He had everyone lined up and had carefully memorized the list of names. For some reason, however, one of the officials stood in the wrong place as a result of which the whole order went awry, so that when my father rattled off the introductions he suddenly realized that he was using the wrong names or, rather, introducing everybody by a false name. I can never decide whether he or the officials were more disconcerted, but Mountbatten didn't seem to notice anything was amiss or, if he did, was far too polite to give any indication to that effect.

Apart from the fun and the festivities, however, Mountbatten's visit had a serious political purpose. The day for the British to depart was rapidly nearing, and while most of the Indian States—by sheer compulsion of geography if nothing else—were making up their minds which of the two new nations to join, there were a few who had still to make their decision. These included the two biggest Indian States, Hyderabad and Kashmir. While Hyderabad was entirely surrounded by territory belonging to the Indian Union, Jammu and Kashmir had boundaries both with the Indian Union and the proposed new State of Pakistan. Further, our State was ethnically diverse and inhabited by Muslims (both Sunni and Shia), Hindus, Buddhists and other religious groups. I suspect that in his heart my father still did not believe that the British would actually leave. Indecisive by nature, he merely played for time.

To be fair to him, of course, the situation he faced was a complex one, and there was no easy option. If he acceded to Pakistan, a large chunk of his people, including his entire Dogra base, would have been outraged. If he acceded to India he risked alienating a large section of his Muslim subjects. Independence could perhaps have been an attractive proposition, but to carry that off would have required careful preparation and prolonged negotiations with the parties concerned, as well as tremendous political and diplomatic ability. Mountbatten in fact had come to persuade my father to make up his mind well before 15 August, and had brought an assurance from the Indian leaders that they would not take objection to his deciding in whatever way he thought fit, even if it was accession to Pakistan.

A typical feudal reaction to a difficult situation is to avoid facing it, and my father was particularly prone to resort to this. Instead of taking advantage of Mountbatten's visit to discuss the whole situation meaningfully and trying to arrive at a rational decision, he first sent the Viceroy out on a prolonged fishing trip to Thricker (where Mountbatten shocked our staff by sunbathing in the nude) and then—having fixed a meeting just before his departure—got out of it on the plea that he had suddenly developed a severe attack of colic. Mountbatten, as has been recorded by his aide Campbell-Johnson, saw through the deception without any difficulty and returned to Delhi. Thus the last real chance of working out a viable political settlement was lost.

Chapter 5

Meanwhile my hip showed no improvement, and ultimately the eminent surgeon Colonel Mirajkar was called in from Lahore. He advised that the hip joint should be immobilized in a plaster cast. The prospect of being confined to bed was highly distasteful, but the pain was getting worse and there was no alternative but to accept the doctor's advice. In June the plaster cast was put on by Mirajkar himself, and I found myself at one stroke converted from a reasonably normal human being into virtually a cripple. For anyone who has not been through the experience, the physical and psychological problems of being confined to bed in plaster for a long period can hardly be imagined. The sheer physical discomfort of the hard cast, which started at my waist and went all the way down the right leg to the toes, was formidable, and the incapacity to move without help even in bed, the itching under the plaster from which there was no possibility of relief, and, above all, the inability to go to the lavatory were a maddening combination.

The nights were the worst. In the day I was lifted out of bed on to a wheel-chair and brought in to sit with my parents and others. They all tried hard to keep me amused, and we would play rummy and ludo. In the evenings some of my cousins would visit me or I would read. But when night fell and I was alone in bed with the dreadful plaster cast, my heart would sink and I had a dreadful feeling of trapped hopelessness. The only consolation came from prayer. My mother had given me a rosary and a picture of Durga—the great goddess riding on a lion—which I kept by my bed. Often I would spend hours telling the beads and sometimes fall asleep with the rosary in my hand. Occasionally I would dream that the whole thing was a nightmare, and that when I awoke I would find myself perfectly fit again. But in the mornings I would awake to the realization that my illness was a grim reality. I think it was in those days that I developed the capacity to come to terms with reality, howsoever unpleasant. I was always introspective, but this enforced and prolonged confinement when boys of my age would be at their most active, drove my mind deeper into itself.

I had been told that the plaster would be on for three months, after which I would be well again and able to resume a normal life. The days lengthened into weeks, the weeks into months. It was 1947, the year in which India was to rise to freedom through an ocean of blood and destruction. Much has been said about the non-violent nature of our freedom struggle, and how we were able to achieve independence without resort to armed conflict. This, of course, is true in the sense that not a drop of British blood was shed in the process, and Gandhiji was certainly a unique leader. But India paid in full measure the bitter price of freedom in the savage and tragic communal conflicts that swept the subcontinent in 1946 and 1947. Hundreds of thousands of innocent men, women and children were sacrificed in the fires of religious hatred and fanaticism as Hindus and Muslims found themselves locked in deadly and unequal struggle—unequal because in all cases it was the minority in any particular city or locality that suffered most. Streams of Hindu and Sikh refugees began to pour into the State from neighbouring Panjab. Jammu and Kashmir had for long been an example of communal harmony, and at a time when the whole of India was aflame it seemed as if the State would remain a haven of peace and tranquillity. This is what Gandhiji meant when he said that in the engulfing darkness the only ray of light seemed to him to come from Kashmir.

Gandhiji in fact visited Srinagar in August that year. There was great excitement when we knew he was coming, and this rose dramatically when we heard that, in disregard of his normal practice, he would come to see my father at the palace. Even my father seemed thrilled, and of course I insisted that I should meet him also. After some discussion it was agreed that my father, my mother and I would meet Gandhiji under one of the Chinar trees in the front lawn of Gulab Bhavan. Special arrangements were made for goat's milk and fruit, and we took our places under the tree an hour before he was due to arrive. At the appointed hour—five in the afternoon of 1 August, if I remember correctly—Gandhiji arrived. My father went to receive him at the porch, and they walked out into the garden to the tree where my mother and I awaited them. I will never forget how moved I was to see that frail figure walking towards us, tiny alongside the tall figure of my father. Here was a man who had become a living legend, who by sheer moral courage had shaken to its foundations the greatest empire the world had ever seen. Though I have a fairly sharp memory I remember hardly anything of the conversation. As he sat down Gandhiji turned to me and said '*Kaise ho*' (how are you?). Then he started a long monologue in a low, lisping voice which I could not clearly follow. My father listened respectfully, but as far as I can recall said hardly anything himself. All I was able to gather from Gandhiji's words was that he was urging my father to ascertain the wishes of his people, to take his people into confidence, and to align himself with rather than against them in the political turmoil that was engulfing the country.

After about ninety minutes Gandhiji got up to go. My mother pressed him to partake of some milk and fruit, but he declined saying that it was not his eating time. At her insistence he agreed to have the fruit put into his car. He left, smiling at me as he said goodbye, dressed in white and with a sad smile which still lingers in my memory. Then he walked back across the lawn followed by both my parents and I was left alone under the tree. I never saw him again in life, but I did see him once in an extraordinarily vivid dream from which his picture still stands in crystal clarity within my mind. But that was several years after he had fallen victim to the assassin's bullets.

Events now began gathering momentum. The British actually seemed to be sincere in their desire to leave by 15 August. It has rightly been said of the British that nothing they did in India became them so much as the manner of their leaving, and it is quite remarkable how all traces of bitterness between us and them disappeared so soon after Independence. This was, of course, largely a tribute to the unique manner in which the Indian National Congress led by Gandhiji conducted the free-dom movement. His doctrine of opposition without hatred, and struggle without violence, was matched by the consummate commonsense and the strong liberal tradition of Britain, parti-cularly under the post-War Labour Government. But with the continuing deadlock between the Congress and the Muslim League, the partition of the subcontinent became inevitable.

The position of the five hundred and odd Indian States re-

mained theoretically ambiguous, because the British took the
view that the rulers were free to accede to either of the new
States that would come into being after they left. However, as
Mountbatten pointed out quite bluntly to the Chamber of
Princes, their choice was in fact virtually dictated by the compulsions of geography. Whenever these were sought to be
violated, as for instance in Junagadh and Hyderabad—both
situated entirely within the Indian Union—the result was a
foregone conclusion. Not so, however, in the case of Jammu and
Kashmir. A bare glance at any map of India at the time is
sufficient to highlight the unique geographical location of this
State, with boundaries that abutted both India and Pakistan,
as also Tibet in the east and separated from the Soviet Union
in the north only by a narrow strip of Afghan territory. I have
mentioned earlier the special British interest in the northern
province of Gilgit, and several historians have built a whole
thesis around the consistent determination of the British to
dominate this crucially strategic area. Indeed as far back as
1935 my father had been pressurized by the British into leasing
the Gilgit Agency to them for sixty years. To add to the com-
plexity of the situation, the State was composed in its various
regions of people belonging to vastly different ethnic, cultural
and religious groups. Thus the valley was inhabited predominantly by Sunni Muslims with a small community of Shias,
Sikhs and the redoubtable Kashmiri Pandits; Jammu predominantly by Dogra Hindus with a significant Muslim component, the western strip from Muzaffarpur to Mirpur by
Panjabi Muslims; Gilgit, Skardu and Kargil by Shia Muslims,
and Ladakh by Lamaistic Buddhists. This extraordinary patch-
work was, of course, the handiwork of my great ancestor
Maharaja Gulab Singh who carved out the State with consummate skill in the middle of the nineteenth century. As long
as the question of Pakistan was merely an academic exercise,
the people of the State remained by and large united in their
loyalty to the ruling family, although Sheikh Abdullah's bitter
anti-Dogra movement in the thirties and forties had succeeded
in making an impression upon politically aware sections in the
Kashmir valley. But once the British intention to withdraw
became established, and the emergence of Pakistan a certainty,
the whole situation underwent a fundamental change. The

State was thrown into inner turmoil; areas bordering the future Pakistani provinces of Panjab and N.W.F.P. started becoming restive, the valley saw the growth of the political movement led by Sheikh Abdullah who was pro-Jawaharlal Nehru but against my father, while the Muslim Conference was pro my father but also pro-Pakistan.

The situation was so complex that even a person far more aware of contemporary realities than my father would have found it virtually impossible to come to a neat, peaceful solution. As I have pointed out, if he had acceded to Pakistan, the Hindu areas of the State would have been virtually liquidated in the wake of the communal frenzy sweeping across north India at the time. If, on the other hand, he had earlier acceded to India he would have run the risk of alienating a large section of his Muslim subjects who constituted seventy-five per cent of the State. In retrospect the only rational solution would appear to have been to take the initiative in promoting and presiding over a peaceful partition of his State between the two new nations. But that would have needed clear political vision and careful planning over many years. As it turned out, the State was, in fact, partitioned, but in a manner that caused untold suffering and bloodshed, poisoning relations between India and Pakistan right down to the present day.

My father's only positive reaction to the rapidly approaching partition was to offer to sign a Standstill Agreement with both the 'Dominions', as they were then called. Pakistan signed the agreement but, soon thereafter, began exerting pressure on the State by interfering with essential supplies. At that time all the major communication systems into the State lay through Pakistan, the road from Kohala and the two railheads at Rawalpindi and Sialkot. Thus Pakistan launched a virtual economic blockade to force my father to accede to it, while India asked for further clarifications before signing the agreement. In a letter replying to a communication from Mehr Chand Mahajan, who had by then taken over as Prime Minister of the State, Jawaharlal Nehru wrote on 20 October 1947:

My dear Mr Mahajan,
    I am in receipt of your letter of the 18th October.
    I am aware of the difficulties Kashmir has had recently, more especially in regard to the attitude adopted by Pakistan towards it.

When you were here last we discussed this matter also. I assured you then that we have the friendliest feelings towards Kashmir and its people and that we would gladly help to the best of our ability in providing Kashmir with the commodities it specially needs. We would like to do so for humanitarian reasons as well as because of our deep interest in the future of the people of Jammu and Kashmir State. Our self-interest also demands this. We are strongly of the opinion that no coercion should be exercised on Kashmir State and its people and that they should be allowed to function in their own way and to make such decisions as they think fit and proper. In the furtherance of this policy we shall direct our efforts.

You will appreciate that there are some difficulties at present in establishing proper communications between India and Kashmir. We hope that these difficulties will be overcome soon by our joint efforts. In regard to sending necessary commodities to Kashmir, we should like to know what exactly you require. You are aware that the situation in India in regard to commodities is also a serious one and many important articles are rationed because of short supply. It is not easy for us to spare them. Nevertheless, we shall try our utmost to send you anything that you particularly need. I understand that salt and kerosene oil are specially needed by your people. Could you kindly let me have some idea of what you require urgently?

Regarding other forms of assistance, you have our good-will but you will appreciate that these will depend on circumstances. I suggest to you that there should be close contact between Kashmir State authorities and our Government so as to ensure co-operation in matters of common concern.

Yours sincerely,
Jawaharlal Nehru

Intelligence reports from the frontier areas of Poonch and Mirpur as well as the Sialkot sector started coming in which spoke of large-scale massacre, loot and rape of our villagers by aggressive hordes from across the borders. I recall the grim atmosphere that began to engulf us as it gradually became clear that we were losing control of the outer areas. My father occasionally handed some of these reports to me and asked me to explain them in Dogri to my mother, and I still recall my embarrassment in dealing with the word 'rape' for which I could find no acceptable equivalent. Meanwhile all my father's Muslim friends seemed to fall away, including 'Bhaijan' Effendi. My personal grapevine told me that he had, before leaving with his family for Rawalpindi, tried desperately to see my father but had been refused permission to enter the palace gates. I like to think that he was making a last effort to help in averting the disaster that was fast closing in upon us.

A new, unfamiliar set of people began appearing at the palace. Ramchandra Kak, the one man who had the intellectual capacity to make some coherent effort towards an acceptable settlement, had been dismissed and humiliated by my father. His place was formally taken by an old Dogra Minister, General Janak Singh Katoch from Kangra, who had served our family with great loyalty for many decades, but it was clear that he was merely a figurehead. Ram Lal Batra appeared from some obscure corner of the Panjab to become Deputy Prime Minister. He had evidently been Dewan in one of the tiny hill States of north India, and his comprehension accurately reflected this background. Yet another person had earlier appeared who was to play a more important role in the events of the next few months—Lala Mehr Chand Mahajan, also from Kangra and who became Prime Minister at this crucial juncture with the blessings of Sardar Patel, although it later became clear that he was not particularly popular with Nehru.

The centre of activity in our house was where my father sat in the lower corridor of the Eastern Wing. After breakfast I was also wheeled in there, my mother came down, the courtiers and advisers assembled and we would sit there throughout the day listening to the radio, sometimes playing ludo, backgammon or rummy. Victor Rosenthal was there, and he did his best to cheer my father up because he had become increasingly withdrawn and hardly ever left the palace. Swami Sant Dev was still ensconced at the Chashmashahi house, but as the situation deteriorated his visits to the palace, and my father's to him, steadily decreased. I think my father had come to realize that the Swami's pretensions to great occult powers were somewhat over-rated, and his old scepticism had begun to reassert itself. But by then it was too late.

The Jammu and Kashmir State Forces, comprising nine infantry battalions, the bodyguard cavalry and two mountain batteries, were strung out in penny packets along the hundreds of miles of State borders from Gilgit down to Mirpur. The forces had an enviable military record at home and abroad ever since they were raised a century earlier by Maharaja Gulab Singh during the founding of the State; its Hindu and Muslim troops, including Dogras from Kangra and Gurkhas from Nepal, had shown exemplary courage and comradeship for many decades. But now a new factor had entered, the grim significance of which was not realized by my father or his advisers. The virus of communalism that was raging in the subcontinent could not have left our State uncontaminated. The main recruiting area for the Muslim component of the forces had been the provinces of Mirpur and Poonch, from where several martial classes of Rajput Muslims also provided thousands of recruits for the Indian Army. With the creation of Pakistan all those regiments opted for that country, and the people of these areas, directly contiguous to the new nation and bound to West Pakistan by bonds of religion and family relationship, were naturally swayed against my father despite their traditional loyalty. Thus not only were the State Forces dangerously over-extended, but one-third had in effect switched loyalty to the other side and were waiting for the opportunity to defect. Added to this was the discontent amounting to revolt in some areas contiguous to Pakistan, and Jinnah's single-minded determination that Kashmir was to be the fairest jewel in the crown of the new State that he had virtually single-handedly carved out of the subcontinent. All that was required to ignite the entire situation was a flaming brand. This came with brutal swiftness in the shape of the infamous tribal invasion of Jammu and Kashmir.

The storm finally broke on 25 October that year. It was Dussehra and, incredibly enough, the annual Darbar was actually held in Srinagar as usual. By then serious trouble had broken out on the borders, and my father had sent Brigadier Rajinder Singh Jamwal, who had taken over from General Scott as Chief of the Army Staff of the Jammu and Kashmir State Forces, to go to Uri and fight 'to the last man and the last bullet'. I happened to be present when my father called him and told him in Dogri that the situation was very serious and that he was to fight the invaders to the finish. Rajinder Singh was a man of few words, and I recall how after getting his instructions he saluted my father and mother, smiled at me, and briskly marched out of the room. What happened next is part of military history, a saga of courage and dedication that will rank with any in the world.

Rajinder Singh left for the border of Uri-Domel on the night of 22 October and, in a series of incredibly brave last-ditch manoeuvres, succeeded in holding the advancing hordes back for three vital days before they could reach Baramulla, thus gaining the critical time that was required for the Instrument of Accession to be signed and the Indian Army to begin arriving by air at Srinagar. Hopelessly outnumbered, his Muslim officers and troops turning hostile, the critically wounded Brigadier insisted that he be left on the roadside with only a revolver in his hand, as he had promised my father that the enemy would advance only over his dead body. He was the first gallantry award winner of independent India, being awarded the Maha Vir Chakra posthumously for his outstanding act of bravery and sacrifice. Just over a hundred years earlier General Zorawar Singh had created military history by the brilliant Dogra campaigns in Central Asia, and Brigadier Rajinder Singh closed the century of Dogra rule by another heroic act. A simple but moving memorial now stands at the spot on the road to Uri where he took his last stand and fell to enemy bullets after his own were expended, as commanded by his ruler. Meanwhile another senior officer, Brigadier Ghansara Singh, Governor of the Northern Province of Gilgit, had been taken prisoner by the Gilgit Scouts which, under their British Commandant, Major Brown, had switched loyalty to Pakistan.

Of all this we learnt only much later. On that fateful day I was left virtually alone in the palace while my father and members of the staff were attending the Darbar in the beautiful hall at the city palace on the Jhelum with its richly decorated papier mâché ceiling. Suddenly the lights went out—the invaders had captured and destroyed the only power house at that time which was at Mahura on the main road from Domel to Srinagar along which the invasion was proceeding. In the pitch darkness I sat quite alone in my room on the wheel chair. After a few minutes the eerie silence was broken by the sudden, blood-chilling howl of jackals. Weirdly the cacophony rose and fell, then rose again into a mad crescendo. Death and destruction were fast approaching Srinagar, our smug world had collapsed around us, the wheels of destiny had turned full circle. Suddenly there was a flurry of activity. The subsequent events are a jumble in my mind—the servants frantically rushing around with petromax lamps, my father's precipitate return from the Darbar ashen-faced and grim, V. P. Menon's dramatic air dash to Srinagar to persuade him to move down to Jammu, my father's reluctance but final agreement in view of Menon's insistence, and then the long, nightmarish exodus from Srinagar late at night on the 27th.

My mother showed tremendous composure and presence of mind in that hour of peril. The wife of the Deputy Prime Minister, Mrs Batra, had several fainting fits, but my mother collected all the ladies and families of the staff, organized their feeding and put them up for the night, aided by my Australian nurse, Mrs Stewart. Finally the convoy began to move. My father drove his own car with Victor Rosenthal at his side and two staff officers with loaded revolvers in the back seat. My mother followed with the ladies in several cars. I was in no position to get into a car because of the heavy plaster cast, so my wheel chair was lifted and placed in the back of one of the station wagons that my father used for his shikar expeditions. It was bitterly cold as the convoy pulled out of the palace in the early hours of the morning. The raiders were pouring in from across the border, pillaging, looting and raping as they came, and there were rumours that the road to Jammu had been cut and that we were likely to be ambushed on the way. There was no armed escort except for the palace guards, and as we left we had only our faith in God to sustain us. The journey was interminable, with numerous stops *en route*. I fell into an uneasy sleep, half hoping that I would awake to the comfort and security of my room and that the whole sequence was only a bad dream. But each time I awoke the night was colder and darker, and suddenly my hip started throbbing with pain.

All through that dreadful night we drove, slowly, haltingly, as if reluctant to leave the beautiful valley that our ancestors had ruled for generations. Our convoy crawled over the 9,000 ft Banihal Pass just as first light was beginning to break. When we stopped at Kud, a small settlement sixty miles from Jammu, we saw that a cream coloured car had joined our grim procession. It was Swami Sant Dev, whose miraculous powers did not include the capacity to face the raiders. Victor told me later that throughout the journey my father spoke not a word as he drove. When the next evening he finally reached Jammu and pulled up at the palace he uttered but one sentence—'We have lost Kashmir'.

The weeks that followed are still blurred in my memory. I continued to be immobilized as my hip had shown no sign of improvement, and as month followed month I began to get the terrible feeling that perhaps I would never be able to walk again and would remain an invalid throughout my life. I continued to maintain a cheerful exterior, which surprised others, but deep inside this gnawing fear grew, and often I would lie awake far into the night with a feeling of helpless anguish. By then the Pakistani invasion was in full swing. The tribals, aided and abetted by Pakistani troops in mufti, had poured into the valley and almost succeeded in reaching Srinagar and capturing the airport. Had they done so, the valley would have been doomed because there was simply not enough time for the Indian Army to move by road. The gallant suicide stand of Rajinder Singh and his men had held the raiders up for three crucial days, thus enabling the historic airlift to get underway. The Indian Air Force and the Indian Army with tremendous courage and sacrifice were able first to save Srinagar by the narrowest of margins and then launch a counter-offensive.

A Brigadier Paranjpye was commanding the troops in the Jammu sector under the overall command of General Kulwant Singh, and they came quite often to the palace for a drink and discussion with my father. The then ruler of Patiala, Maharaja Yadavendra Singh, also came with a contingent of the Patiala State forces. He was a fine figure of a man, standing six foot six in his turban, but his mien was gentle and he talked in a pleasant voice which belied his formidable exterior. Phrases like 'l of c' (line of communications), 'H.Q.' (Headquarters), 'P.O.L.' (petrol, oil and lubricants), 'C.O.' (Commanding Officer) began to figure increasingly in the conversation. In the Jammu Province the invaders had made important advances; Mirpur, Bhimbar, Rajouri, all border towns of considerable importance, had fallen, and the crucial town of Poonch had been besieged. Although maintaining outward composure, with news of each reverse my father would wince inwardly as if something had died within him. Only on one occasion, when the twin villages of Deva and Batala which were the home of the Chib and Bhau Rajputs fell, did I see a hint of tears in his eyes.

My mother was very active in refugee relief work. Thousands of men, women and children were pouring into Jammu from the areas under Pakistani occupation, and were given food and shelter in a number of refugee camps in and around the city. These, of course, were the lucky ones. Many thousands perished in the butchery and carnage that accompanied the invasion. There was hardly any family which did not lose half or more of its members in the slaughter, and there were numerous cases of only a single child escaping from a joint family. The misery and suffering were unspeakable, and it was at this moment that my mother's courage and her surprisingly strong organizing capacity was revealed. She would often spend the entire day visiting one camp after another, distributing rations and clothes deep into the night. Often she financed and arranged for simple marriages among the refugees, thus bringing some comfort to the shattered families. Indeed she and her band of workers began to be looked upon as angels of mercy, and to this day there are people who recall the tremendous services she rendered to the destitute and terrified refugees at that time. She also organized a women's volunteer force known as the Maharani Seva Dal, and arranged for them to receive paramilitary training from the army authorities. This was the second time she had thrown herself into relief work, the first being in the War Aid Committee during the Second World War, and it seems that this sort of situation brought out the best in her. In contrast, my father rarely left the palace during those days, although my mother did succeed in dragging him on rare occasions to a refugee camp or a Seva Dal function.

By far the most memorable encounter for me during that period was my first meeting with Jawaharlal Nehru. On his first visit to Jammu he had come briefly to the palace but been very busy, and I complained to my father of not having had the opportunity to meet him. The second time he came my father brought him into my room. It was a great moment to meet the man who had become something of an idol for me. As he entered the room I was struck by two things, the agility with which he moved and that unforgettable smile—pensive yet intensely human. My father introduced me by saying 'Tiger is your great admirer'. He asked how I was, and good-naturedly apologized for not having seen me on his first visit. I was too overwhelmed to say anything very intelligent and simply asked him to autograph my copy of his *Autobiography*. He was in the room for barely three minutes, but the moment remains with me.

Sardar Vallabhbhai Patel also visited Jammu on two or three occasions, accompanied by the Secretary for States, V. P. Menon, and in fact it was he who realized that at the rate I was going there was little chance of my ever recovering. He suggested that I be sent to America for treatment, a proposition that at first was violently opposed by my mother. The Sardar was particularly considerate to and friendly with my parents, and finally he and my father were able to persuade my mother to agree. I welcomed the idea, not only because of the hope it held out for my recovery but also because I was finding the whole atmosphere of tension and conflict extremely depressing and yearned to get away.

The Sardar arranged for a special foreign exchange allocation to meet the expenses for my treatment, and it was decided that I would be accompanied by Brigadier N. S. Rawat, a senior Gurkha officer of the State Forces, and Captain Ranjit Singh, one of my father's aides. Victor Rosenthal, being my father's only friend with contacts in the U.S.A., was asked to initiate inquiries and make arrangements for my admission to a suitable hospital in New York. He was able to do this within a few weeks, and finally the date for my departure from Jammu was fixed in the last week of December. Before I left I asked my mother to distribute all my clothes to refugee children. I had grown out of them while in bed and there didn't seem much point in storing them. I left the palace in the evening because of an auspicious timing, and spent the night in the Satwari Cantonment. Before I left, my mother bade me a tearful farewell; my father was also moved but, of course, kept up a stern facade. Although none of us said so, at the back of our minds was an unspoken dread that we may never see each other again.

The chartered DC-3 took almost a whole day to reach Bombay, and two days later on 29 December the three of us—

Rawat, Ranjit and I—boarded a four-engined T.W.A. Sky-master at Bombay airport. I was driven up to the plane in an ambulance, then lifted into the cabin and placed on two seats with several cushions in between to make up a sort of bed. I remember the curious feeling I had as I was being lifted up the steps; sorrow at leaving my country mingled with a sense of excitement at the unknown journey that stretched out before me. The American crew entered the plane soon after, and the Captain came and asked how I was. The plane took off around five in the evening. Our first stop was somewhere in the Gulf area, and the second in Cairo. From there we flew on to Rome where we landed in a blinding rainstorm. Passengers kept getting in and out, but I was quite unable to move and watched the proceedings from my window. We then flew on to Paris, which we reached after dark, the city an illuminated carpet from the air. From Paris we went on to Shannon in Ireland and from there started the Atlantic crossing which, in those days of propeller aircraft, seemed interminable. The shortest route between two land points was from Shannon to Gander in New-foundland, and even that took the better part of a whole day. We reached Gander towards sundown, and from there made the final hop to New York.

New York had just had its heaviest snowfall in sixty years, and when we landed late in the evening of 31 December there was over two feet of snow in the city. The doors of our plane opened to let in piercingly cold winds. Victor Rosenthal's representative, a Mrs Toole, was at the airport, and after long formalities were completed an ambulance drove up to the plane, a stretcher brought into the cabin, and I was lifted on to it and carried down into the vehicle. A news photographer was there to record my arrival. Ranjit sat with me, Mrs Toole in front with the driver, and we started off on our long drive into town, siren screeching and the snowfall reducing visibility to a few feet.

Thus it was, as 1947 came to its close, that I found myself half a world away from home in a strange country, seeing snow-fall for the first time in my life, since I had never spent a winter in Kashmir. As the ambulance sped towards its destination my mind went back over the experiences of my life so far—my childhood, school and the frenetic events of the last two years.

Would I ever see India again, or my parents? What would become of the State of which I was born heir apparent? Would I ever be able to walk again, or was I condemned to be a helpless cripple for the rest of my life? At that moment the prospect appeared to be one of unrelieved gloom. The only thing that kept me going was the mantra for worship of the Goddess that my mother had taught me several years earlier, and which she had earnestly enjoined upon me never to forget in times of need and distress. She had also given me a small picture of Durga *Singhavahini*, the eight-armed Goddess riding on a lion, a powerful symbolic representation of the divine astride material power. Throughout the long flight I had clutched it, and in that hour of despondence it provided my only comfort.

We were now entering New York, and I got the first glimpse of the great city that was to be my home for much longer than I realized, its huge buildings thrusting up into the raging blizzard, their tops lost in the swirling snow. After a drive of almost two hours the ambulance finally pulled up at 321 East 42nd Street where stood the Hospital for Special Surgery. It was late at night and at first the institution seemed to be deserted, but soon someone appeared and I was lifted out of the ambulance into the hospital veranda, and wheeled into a lift. Then, at the fifth floor, the lift stopped and I was wheeled along to the end of the corridor into Room 509. By the time I was transferred to my bed and the ambulance attendants departed it was getting on to midnight. They all had New Year parties to attend, and were understandably in a hurry to get away. Ranjit was in Room 508 next to mine, and he also went to his room for a while. At last I found myself alone, with the picture of Durga and a photograph of my parents on the high table next to my hospital bed. I heard in the distance the sound of a great clock striking the midnight hour. A new year had begun and, for me, a new life.

Chapter 6

America is an astonishing country, even when viewed by a teenage Indian from a hospital room. There was something different about the whole atmosphere, an air of freshness and informality. To begin with, the nurses, doctors and ward attendants looked at me with frank curiosity, as a photograph of my arrival had been published in the *Daily Mirror*. All sorts of odd stories had evidently been circulating about Indian princes, and so when they heard I had checked into the hospital they probably expected to see some kind of freak. They were all very friendly and seemed pleasantly surprised that I could speak English. In fact I spoke it better than most of them, and it was several weeks before my ear became accustomed to the curious American accent and what struck me as quaint usages, such as 'crackers' for biscuits and 'cookies' for pastries.

I was visited by Dr Philip D. Wilson the day after I arrived. Dr Wilson was one of the most distinguished orthopaedic surgeons in America at the time, and, like some of the really great doctors, his very presence infused a sense of confidence in the patient. He asked me several questions and then gave directions that the plaster cast on my leg should be removed and the usual battery of X-ray, blood and other tests taken so that he could decide on a line of treatment. The cast was replaced by an eight-pound traction on my foot to keep the joint in position. After months in the cast my knee and ankle were quite stiff, and I could not move the hip joint at all. To help loosen the joints I was taken every morning to a heated swimming pool in the hospital which specialized in treating muscular atrophy. Getting into the water for the first time after six months was a pleasant experience, and I found I could move around with ease. Gradually I started putting weight on my legs, and a few days later was allowed to stand in my room with the help of crutches, an extraordinary feeling after lying flat for half a year.

Soon after arrival we bought a radio, and I was fascinated by the large number of stations available and also the fact that the

Hotel Martinez, Cannes

The author with his mother, 1931

The author's parents in procession at Jammu, 1931

The author with his father, 1935

On horseback, 1936

The author with
Digby and Bilti,
1936

In ceremonial
clothes, 1938

About to inaugurate an exhibition: the author with N. Gopalaswami Ayyangar
and Colonel K. N. Haksar, 1939

The author's mother in
Dogri dress, 1940

His parents, 1942

Karan Nivas, Srinagar

Amar Mahal, Jammu

Churchill's War Cabinet: standing fourth from left is Maharaja Hari Singh

Boat procession on the Jhelum; the author and his father are in the first boat

Swami Sant Dev and Thakur
Nachint Chand, 1945

The author on his sixteenth
birthday, 1947

The sacred thread ceremony, 1949

With Jawaharlal
Nehru, 1949

With Jawaharlal
Nehru at the first
convocation of
Jammu and
Kashmir University,
1949

The bridegroom, 1950

The author's mother,
1950

Maharaja Hari Singh,
1950

The wedding ceremony, 1950

The author and his wife after
the reception, 1950

With Sheikh Abdullah
in Jammu, 1950

At Chushul airport: with Jawaharlal Nehru, Indira Gandhi, Sheikh Abdullah and others, 1951

At Chushul with Jawaharlal Nehru, 1951

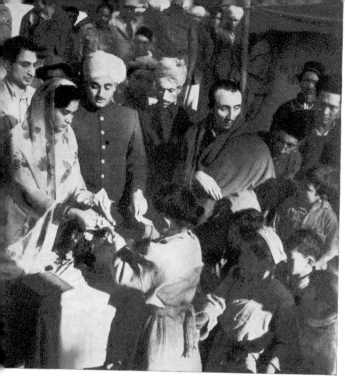

At Leh, 1951

At Srinagar airport with Indira Gandhi, Edwina Mountbatten,
Jawaharlal Nehru and Sheikh Abdullah, 1951

The author being sworn in as Sadar-i-Riyasat, 1952

programmes went on for eighteen hours, from six in the morning
to midnight. There was a bewildering array of music, plays,
talks, news and sports commentaries, from which I soon chose
my favourite items, mainly pop music. In fact music once again
played a vital role in a very trying period of my life, and although it was poles apart from Indian classical music I discovered that in whatever form, music has the unique capacity
to soothe the mind and prevent it from slipping into depression
or worse. Later, a television set was also acquired, which added
a new dimension to my life in hospital. There were two additional attractions. One was a weekly film show on the third
floor for patients who were in a position to be moved, and the
second a solarium on the sixth floor—a large, glass-panelled
room with many potted plants and trees. It was marvellous to
be able to go up there and savour the warmth of the sun without
being exposed to the chill fury of the snow.

The unusual friendliness of the Americans became evident
soon after I arrived. Not only did the entire hospital staff go
out of its way to be pleasant, but several visitors began coming
in to see me, including some old Indian contacts and friends of
Rosenthal's. Among them were a middle-aged couple, Norris
and Dorothy Harkness, and an old India hand, Major John
Nethersole and his wife Arlene. Looking back, I find it amazing
how much all of them did to befriend me. They would drop in
every two or three days, bring sweets and 'cookies', and sit with
me for hours chatting away or playing card games and backgammon. The women in particular seemed to develop an
almost motherly affection for me. I wonder whether the fact
that I was missing my mother so much in some way conveyed
itself to them.

Meanwhile the Kashmir dispute in the United Nations was
in the front pages of all the U.S. newspapers. The wily Zafarul-
lah Khan, Pakistan's able chief delegate, seemed to our utter
exasperation to be getting the better of the Indian delegation
led by no less a person than the former Prime Minister of
Jammu and Kashmir, Sir Gopalaswami Ayyangar. The latter
came to see me in hospital one day, soon after the shocking news
of Mahatma Gandhi's assassination on 30 January, a tired and
broken man. Another member on the Indian delegation who
also visited me was Sheikh Mohammad Abdullah. Having

5

heard so much about him since my childhood I was quite excited by his visit, and, indeed, he was an impressive figure of a man, six foot four and well built. It was curious that a man with whom I was to develop such intimate political relations met me for the first time half a world away from our home State.

Despite all these visits and diversions, the fact remained that I was still a cripple, unable to move on my own, still miserably dependent upon sponge baths and bedpans. After studying my X-rays and bringing in two more specialists for consultation, Dr Wilson decided by the end of January that, while an operation was not immediately necessary, they would try a manipulation and replastering of the hip joint. Thus began the first of a whole series of encounters with anaesthesia. For those who have not undergone this voluntary loss of consciousness there may appear nothing very special about it, but anyone who has will testify that the prospect of going through a belt of unconsciousness is not a pleasant one. However, my main concern was not so much the unconsciousness itself as the horrifying thought that I might awake in the middle of the operation. Each time I would tell the anaesthetist to make quite sure that I remained under until the operation was over.

Two main fears that I had about anaesthesia were that I might lose my mental agility or my virility. Each time I would come round after an operation I would check as to whether I was still mentally alert by—oddly enough—trying to recall the definition of 'optimum population' that I had learnt for my Intermediate economics examination. There was no special reason for my having chosen this particular mental formula to test myself, but it is a strange coincidence that a quarter of a century later I was to be involved in framing a National Population Policy. The test for my other fear would have to wait for a few days until the pain of the operation had subsided.

The process of treatment, plastering and replastering went on for several months, as the freezing New York winter gradually changed into a hot and sticky summer. I had picked up several hit tunes from the radio, but, in addition, I decided to start taking chess lessons and also re-establishing some contact with the academic world. For chess it was arranged that a man called Boris Siff would come thrice a week. He was very good, and introduced me to new dimensions of this fascinating game.

On the other three days a Mr J. E. Brown (I am sure it was an assumed name, because he spoke with a gentle Central European accent) came from Columbia University to give lessons in economics and political science. He was very leftist in his leanings, and a strong critic of the American capitalist system. It was he who first put before me the theory that American munition manufacturers were actively involved in fomenting wars in various places in South America so that their wares could retain their regular and highly lucrative markets.

As the weeks went by I began to realize that my hopes for an early recovery in America were steadily receding. Meanwhile events were moving fast in Jammu and Kashmir. The tribal invasion had developed into virtually a full-scale war, in which the State Forces and the Indian Army were pitted against the tribals and regular units of the Pakistan Army. My father's letters gave me news of the military campaign, from which I gathered that the Indian offensive was gradually succeeding in pushing the invaders back. Town after town was recaptured, but the process was much slower than we had hoped. Politically also, changes were taking place. Mehr Chand Mahajan had left the State, and my father had set up by proclamation an Emergency Administration headed by Sheikh Abdullah. It was quite clear that this had been done at the instance of Jawaharlal Nehru. Indeed, after the Instrument of Accession was signed and the Indian Army moved in, effective authority had in fact passed from my father's hands, though this was not formalized till later.

The Constitution of India was also being framed at the time. In one of his letters my father wrote prophetically, 'I have no idea of how the new Constitution for India is going to affect us beyond the fact that before very long the Rulers will disappear even in name'. In hospital I looked eagerly through the gigantic daily newspapers for news about India, which was sparse and unsatisfactory. The size of American newspapers never ceased to surprise me, specially the Sunday edition of the *New York Times* which, with its numerous supplements, sometimes reached two hundred pages. I was an avid reader, and lapped up a great deal of information and new ideas.

Although immobilized due to the plaster cast, I found both my body and mind growing almost visibly, the former mainly because I drank vast quantities of delicious homogenized milk. On my seventeenth birthday we had a party in the hospital, and my photograph receiving the birthday cake from Dr Wilson flanked by my two nurses and a Chinese fellow patient, Tai Loong Yang, was published next day on the front page of the *New York Times*. The report ended with the following cryptic paragraph: 'Sir Hari Singh has recently liberalized his formerly despotic government and his son is said to have democratic ideas. The youth declined, however, to discuss any political matter.' I also did my first radio broadcast at about this time on a show called 'Junior Reporter' in which teenagers discussed the topic of the day. In my intervention I said I hoped India would soon assume her rightful place among the great nations of the world, that the responsibility of the future world rested on its youth and that we should all strive for better understanding and brotherly love.

Looking back I realize that the American interlude with its totally new environment provided my mind the opportunity to break out of the feudal trappings of the State and absorb a different and much freer atmosphere. 1948 happened to be an election year, and I followed closely in the press and on TV the astonishing American electoral process, including the Democratic Convention at which Hubert Humphry, Harold Stassen and others made an unsuccessful bid to wrest the nomination from President Truman, and the Republican session where Thomas Dewey was chosen in an atmosphere of euphoria. The cheer-leaders, bands and the *tamasha* at these conventions amazed me, but Mr Brown kept pointing out that behind all the noise and festivities there were hard-nosed professionals representing various interests who would see to it that neither party strayed too far from the path of capitalism and 'free enterprise'.

The letters I wrote to my father at the time were full of the Security Council proceedings regarding the Kashmir dispute, and questions about the progress of the military campaign in the State. In reply he would give me the salient developments, mentioning specially the recapture of any important town. Surprisingly, he still kept up his interest in the Bombay races as his letters often complained about his trainer and the poor performance of his horses. I also wrote regularly to my mother in

Hindi, and she would reply on her salmon pink paper in an almost undecipherable hand. She had never undergone any formal education, and though in conversation and even in public speeches she was impressive, writing was never her strong point.

Despite the prolonged immobilization of my hip in plaster, now almost a full year since it had first been treated by Dr Mirajkar in Srinagar, the joint did not respond to Dr Wilson's satisfaction. On 6 July Dr Wilson came into my room and said that he had decided to operate upon me the next morning. Evidently the decision had been taken several days earlier, and my father's permission secured, but it had been kept from me so that I would not worry and fret. The conspiracy of silence worked well, because I only had a few hours to worry before the big event. The operation that took place the next morning was much more serious that any of us had realized. It involved a semi-circular incision twelve inches long, and permanent immobilization of the hip joint through a bone graft and a six-inch metal pin. I was on the operation table for several hours, and regained consciousness only late that afternoon. The next five days were the worst that I could ever recall till then. My body was shaken by convulsions caused by the severance of the major hip muscle, the pain was excruciating and with each convulsion the whole bed would shake. I had to have sixteen injections every day—eight of pencillin and eight for the pain, and was given five 250 c.c. bottles of blood by transfusion. If heaven or hell actually exist outside one's consciousness, I think I got a fair approximation of the latter during those terrible post-operation days.

Ranjit was in my room almost round the clock and, along with the three nurses who came for eight hours each, did everything possible to try and lessen my agony. The anaesthesia left a peculiarly unpleasant aftertaste, and I totally lost my appetite. In any case, I was hardly in a position to eat, and was on liquid diet for a week. It was only casually, a few days later, that one of the nurses broke the news of the pin in my hip. My heart sank; I realized then that I would never be able to walk normally again, and indeed at that point was virtually convinced that I would never be able to walk at all. My faith and such courage as I had been able to muster were sorely tested,

and it was only with a supreme effort of will that I resisted
breaking down completely.

Dr Wilson, though, was happy with the operation, and assured me that all would be well in another few months. The
fact that to this day I can play tennis and undertake prolonged
election tours without any discomfort is a tribute to the pro-
fessional competence of that great surgeon, one of the most
distinguished names in the history of orthopaedic surgery. He
would sit by my bed, telling me in a fatherly manner how he
had used the bone graft from the newly developed bone bank.
He also gave me a replica of the special alloy pin that had been
inserted in my hip, which remains with me as a rather gruesome
reminder of one of the critical periods in my life.

I was young and, evidently, stronger than I realized. My first
post-operative letter to my father was scrawled on 14 July,
exactly a week after the operation, and on the 19th I wrote him
a seven-page epistle. By then my wound had begun healing, and
the twenty-five stitches removed. Slowly, very slowly, the pain
subsided and my appetite returned. The vibrancy of youth
began to assert itself, and I think the fact that I refused to go
into a psychological depression made a big difference. Everyone
we knew in New York and in the hospital was most kind and
affectionate; during the several months I had been there I had
made more friends than I realized, and my room was always
full of flowers and 'candy'. As I rigorously concealed my pain
and distress as far as possible, I got the reputation of being
brave and courageous. Even my father in his next letter wrote:
'You have patiently gone through a very great deal of trouble
bravely. . . . I am really proud of you.' High praise, indeed,
coming from him.

For two months I wore a heavy plaster cast and then in
September, after Dr Wilson returned from his summer holiday,
he had the cast removed and a smaller, lighter one applied. The
operation wound had healed perfectly by then, and I remember
vividly the first day that I was allowed to stand after months in
bed. The sensation was so strange that I felt giddy and almost
fell. I was made to stand for longer periods each day, and to
take the first tentative steps in the hospital room, virtually re-
learning how to walk. On 24 September I was well enough to
be able to leave the hospital for the first time in nine months

and go for a short drive in an open car. I was taken down in a wheel chair and lifted into the car. Never will I forget the sheer joy of that first drive in New York city. Those tremendous buildings soaring up into the air were quite overwhelming, and I had a peculiar sensation of sensory distortion, of being suddenly transported into a new dimension of space and time. After the long, dreary months in hospital the very thought that I could once again move around was delicious.

During these months my chess and political science sessions continued. I also started (but did not complete) a Pelmanism course by correspondence with Bombay, and a Speed-writing course which involved a method of condensed writing without using any shorthand. I watched television ardently, followed closely the Presidential campaign with Truman and Dewey criss-crossing the country making unending speeches. Although everyone seemed to think that the rather square Dewey was certain to win, it struck me that Truman had more vigour and fight in him. I read a great deal, books on contemporary politics as well as novels.

News from home remained disturbing. My father was very guarded in his letters—he had warned us that censorship was in the air—but it was clear that although he had been forced by Jawaharlal Nehru to hand over effective power to Sheikh Abdullah, who headed the 'Emergency Administration' and later became Prime Minister, their mutual relations were tense and antagonistic. For example, in a letter dated 18 September he wrote:

The present government was very eager to take over the State Forces under their control. I strongly opposed this move on their part as the Army was a reserved subject. The matter was referred to the States Ministry and I was invited by Sardar Patel to come to Delhi for discussions. After a long discussion, contrary to the wishes of Sheikh Abdullah it was decided that the control of the State Forces should be handed over to the Indian Army for the time being. I would continue to be Commander-in-Chief.

My mobility gradually increased. I began walking with crutches and, accompanied by Ranjit, would walk out of the hospital and down to the corner drug store for ice cream. I was also able to walk into the ground floor of the *Daily News* building on 42nd Street where a huge revolving globe was set in a room full of time charts, news flashes and maps. It was a fascinating place, and I became a regular visitor, spending as many as two or three hours there at a stretch. I had bought myself a couple of suits, ties and a felt hat, and was able to send back some photographs to my parents who were delighted to see how I had grown. Meanwhile, the American Presidential election moved to its climax. Truman scored a stunning upset victory against Dewey, and I won ten dollars off one of the doctors who had given me ten to one against the incumbent President winning.

Although I was gradually improving, I had no illusions about a rapid or complete recovery. In one of my letters to my father I wrote: 'The loosening and strengthening of the muscles of my right leg will be a long slow process, but once I get rid of the plaster permanently it will only be a matter of time. Of course, as you know, my right hip will always be stiff, but after some practice and adjustment in my way of walking and sitting, I do not think that should trouble me too much in life. It will, however, take some time to get used to it.' On 1 November the plaster cast was finally removed, and I was able to restart going into the pool. It was marvellous getting into warm water again, free of that dreadful cast. The competent silver-haired physiotherapist, Miss Helen Clark, who had treated me regularly ever since I entered hospital, gave me underwater massage, as a result of which my right hip and leg gradually began to recover some strength. Dr Wilson was so pleased with my progress that he said I could leave the hospital after a few days and stay in a hotel for another two months so as to be able to come in for physiotherapy and observation by him. So at last on 15 November, exactly 10½ months since I had been carried into the Hospital for Special Surgery, I moved out to the Barclay Hotel, 111 East 48th Street.

In one of his poems Byron suggests that even a prisoner who stays in a single cell long enough becomes attached to the jail. Certainly I had developed a good deal of affection for the hospital—the nurses, the ward staff, the doctors, the fellow patients. Although I suffered physically a great deal there, the atmosphere of affection and consideration helped sustain me. It was in fact quite a wrench to leave, and I was given a royal send off by the entire hospital. Twenty years later, in 1967, I visited New York again as Minister for Tourism and Civil Aviation of the Government of India. The old hospital on 42nd Street had by then been pulled down, and the institution moved in a much more modern and slick building further up town. Dr Wilson, still vigorous and ruddy at eighty, showed me proudly around the gleaming new premises. And yet, somehow, I missed the old.

The Barclay was a spacious and comfortable hotel, not nearly as luxurious as the Waldorf Astoria close by, but well suited to the comparatively limited dollar remittances that my father was allowed to send for my treatment. I particularly enjoyed the luxury of having hot baths again after so many months. To this day I offer up a silent prayer of thanksgiving whenever I sink back into a tub of hot water, and remind myself of how breezily we tend to take the comforts of life for granted until they are denied to us. I was still walking on crutches when I moved into the hotel, but soon started getting around with the help of two canes. Thrice a week I would go to the hospital pool for underwater muscle therapy, while on the other three days Miss Clark would come to the hotel and give me an hour's massage. I was now able to get into taxis and so, along with Rawat and Ranjit, began to take in the sights and sounds and food of New York.

It is truly an incredible city, brighter at night than in the day. Times Square and Broadway were particularly impressive, with thousands of neon signs bursting forth in a permanent burst of light. The huge cinema advertisements fascinated me. *Joan of Arc* had just been released with Ingrid Bergman in the title role, and a gigantic cut-out of her stood higher than any building I had seen in India. We saw this and a number of other movies, including *The Three Musketeers* (with Gene Kelley, Lana Turner, June Allyson and Angela Lansbury), *Enchantment* (David Niven) and *The Paleface* (Bob Hope, Jane Rusell). We were also able to see some plays on Broadway: *Mister Roberts* (with Henry Fonda), Noel Coward's *Private Lives* (with Tallulah Bankhead), *Harvey* (starring a huge, invisible white rabbit) and a comedy *Where's Charley?* (with Ray Bolger).

In addition to movies and plays we went to the top of the

Empire State Building, visited the impressive Rockefeller Centre, shopped at Saks and Macys, admired the famous Rockettes at Radio City Music Hall, witnessed an ice hockey match at Madison Square Garden, cautiously explored the out-skirts of Central Park, and discovered a number of excellent eating places including several Indian restaurants and one called The Barberry Room (19 East 52nd Street) with a starry ceiling and the most comfortable chairs in New York. Just being in the city was an exhilarating experience, specially after having been laid up for eighteen months, and those weeks in New York out of hospital were among the happiest in my life. We also took an overnight train journey to Buffalo from where we went to the Canadian border to see the Niagara Falls.

1948 had drawn to an end, and, unlike the previous New Year's eve when I had been driven in an ambulance along deserted streets, this time we celebrated it in Times Square along with half a million New Yorkers. It was bitterly cold, but we were in high spirits when the clock struck twelve and every-one went berserk. Soon thereafter we found ourselves in an Indian restaurant nearby, where the proprietor served us steam-ing cups of saffron tea. I had heard from several friends, in-cluding Gurubachan Singh of our Foreign Service who was posted there, that Washington was a beautiful city, and so I asked my father for permission to visit it for a week. He agreed, and we went there just in time for President Truman's Inau-gural Parade on 20 January 1949 for which we got tickets through Gurubachan's good offices. Our Ambassador, Shri Rama Rau (whose brother Sir B. N. Rao had been my father's Prime Minister) was out of town, but his gracious wife, Lady Dhanwantri Rama Rau and their daughter, Mrs Premila Wagle, took good care of us. Washington is indeed a lovely city, specially its public memorials. The classical Greek severity of the Lincoln Memorial, with its huge brooding statue of the greatest President, contrasted sharply with the less formal and more intimate Jefferson Memorial set amidst pools and flower-ing bushes. We also went to Mount Vernon to visit George Washington's ancestral home. Both the unrelenting glamour of New York and the classic dignity of Washington, so different from each other, made a powerful impression upon me.

Now that I was improving, my parents began wanting me to

come home, and in my letters to my father I began zeroing in on two major questions that would confront me when I returned. The first was my marriage, which I presumed—erroneously as it turned out—would be to Shanti with whom I had begun corresponding from hospital. I wrote to my father saying that while I appreciated their desire for an early marriage, 'I am sorry that I will not be able to see more of Shanti and get to know her a little better before we are married, because I am sure that if two people know each other well there is more chance of a successful marriage than if they are almost strangers.' The second matter was about my future education, and here I was emphatic enough to read my father a virtual sermon:

I would like you to know that I am very keen to continue my studies up to B.A. and further, that I sincerely believe, and I am sure you do too, that in these rapidly changing times a sound education (in my case subjects such as Economics, Law, etc.) is essential. It is not enough to be born into a high position. I believe that one should be, in these times, capable enough and well enough equipped educationally to make a mark for oneself regardless of any accident of birth in a high position.

Dr Wilson was happy with the way my leg was improving, and it was finally decided that I could leave for home in the first week of February, stopping for a few days each at London and Paris on the return journey. One of the last things we did in New York was to pay a visit to Roosevelt House at Hyde Park along with one of the late President's sons, Eliott Roosevelt and his wife Faye, who had been an actress. We happened to be there on the birth anniversary of the late President, whom I always greatly admired, and we participated in a short memorial service at Arlington Cemetery where he is buried. We were greeted and shown around by his widow, Mrs Eleanor Roosevelt, a woman of great drive and personality. In her column in the *New York World Telegram* on 2 February she recorded our visit and added: 'The young Prince of Kashmir, who has been in this country for an operation, is returning home in a few days to complete his final two years in college. It is his desire later to serve in the United Nations and help to build a peaceful world.'

The return trip to India was in sharp contrast to the grim journey to New York over a year earlier. We boarded a Pan American flight across the Atlantic as Air-India had not yet started plying on this sector. The first stop was London, where we stayed at what had been my father's favourite hotel, the Savoy. Characteristically, he had sent me a meticulously prepared list of clothes I should buy, along with the shops that he himself used to patronize as a young man. Captain and Mrs Wreford came up from the country to see me, and several friends of my father also called. The only trip into the country was to the public school at Charterhouse to meet Shanti's younger brother, Ranbir Singh. The Savoy theatre had just begun showing the celebrated *Mousetrap*, Agatha Christie's all-time theatrical record-breaker, which we saw with interest.

After about a week in London we proceeded to Paris where Victor Rosenthal had laid on a lavish welcome. Two of his brother's grandsons—Jean and Hubert—who were about my age showed me around town, but I was far too shy and self-conscious about my cane to be able to really enjoy myself. The Galeries Lafayette was the most beautifully decorated department store I had ever seen. We visited two famous night-clubs, Lido and Moulin Rouge, and at one restaurant heard Edith Piaf singing. There was some talk of visiting my birthplace in Cannes, but my father was keen that I should not tarry too long on the way home, and so we dropped the idea.

Finally, in the third week of February, we set out on the last lap of the flight back to Bombay. I returned with mixed feelings. I had set out from home over a year ago as a helpless invalid, and though I was now able to get around on my own I had not fully been restored to normal health despite Dr Wilson's assurance that gradually I would be able to play tennis again. In addition, there had been ominous hints in letters from home that politically things were not going well as far as our family was concerned. Besides, the whole question of my forthcoming marriage was in some ways disturbing. It was, therefore, with a sense of foreboding that I awaited the descent of our plane to Bombay late in the evening.

Chapter 7

The welcome I received on my return only heightened my fears. Instead of the enthusiastic greeting that I expected, an old friend of my father, Fatehsingji of Limbdi (Uncle Fatty) met us at the foot of the ladder and said that I must come quietly with him to a car in which my father was waiting for me. Evidently they had received some sort of assassination threat, and were afraid of giving undue publicity to my arrival. Once in the car we sped off to 19 Nepean Road which my father had bought some years ago from the Modys. It was very odd meeting my father after so long under such circumstances. When we reached the house, my mother, who was recovering from an operation for piles, rose to greet me and clasped me to her bosom. I was home at last after almost fourteen months, but all I felt after the long flight was tiredness and a strange sense of let down. As soon as we got to the house my father, who was always impatient when it came to something in which he was interested, asked me to unpack and show him the things we had bought under his instructions in America. Those included shaving equipment, cigarette lighters and other mechanical and electrical gadgets that gave him great pleasure because of his curiously inventive turn of mind. I had also bought some perfume and other cosmetics for my mother. From the next morning, however, grim and disturbing tidings began coming in. I learnt that the political situation in the State was very bad, and that there was tremendous tension between my father, who was now virtually a constitutional figurehead, and Sheikh Abdullah who, with Jawaharlal Nehru's support, was heading the State administration as Prime Minister and wielded executive power. The old bitterness between the Dogras and the Kashmiris had surfaced again with the dramatic reversal of their roles after a century of Dogra rule. Although, as I have recorded, my father was not really interested in exercising political or administrative power, he was understandably jealous of his authority and prestige as Maharaja, and deeply resented the manner in which Jawaharlal had made his handing over power to Sheikh Abdullah a virtual condition for extending military aid to save the State from Pakistani occupation. This marked for me the beginning of a deep conflict between loyalty to my father who, I realized, represented a system and mode of thought rapidly becoming obsolete in free India, and regard for Jawaharlal Nehru, who was my political guru and whom I greatly admired.

Another startling development that I learnt of soon after I returned was that my father had decided that Shanti was not really a suitable bride for me, and wanted to break off the engagement. There was really no justification for this, but then the engagement itself had been an absurd move based on one of my father's mood-cum-impulse decisions that defied rational analysis. I had no say in the engagement decision, and although this time the matter was put to me for my views I realized that my father had already made up his mind and there was little I could do to change it. I had not seen Shanti at all since her visit to Srinagar several years earlier, and although we had corresponded while I was in America I had to admit that I did not have any emotional involvement. So the decision was taken, grossly unfair as it was to the Ratlam family, and an emissary sent to Ratlam for the purpose. Incredibly, my father had the nerve to ask for the return of the jewellery he had given Shanti at the betrothal ceremony. By then the old Maharaja Sajjan Singhji was dead and Shanti's brother, Lokeshwar Singh, was the titular ruler. It gave me some grim satisfaction when he bluntly refused to return the jewellery.

I learnt soon what lay behind these strange developments. During the Hyderabad operations a military contingent had been sent to India as a gesture of goodwill and friendship by the Rana Prime Minister of Nepal, Maharaja Mohun Shumsher, under the command of his elder son General Sarada Shumsher. At a wedding in Delhi between the Raja of Khetri and Princess Bhuvan, daughter of the Nepalese Ambassador General Singha who was a younger brother of the Prime Minister, my parents had met General Sarada, his wife and their children. The eldest child was a girl, Yasho Rajya Lakshmi, then barely twelve years old. Apparently it was Sardar Patel who hinted that a matrimonial alliance between the ruling families of Kashmir and Nepal might have valuable political implications for the new India that he was so painstakingly building up. At least this is what I was told, though I never was able to get the matter verified. In any case, the timely appearance of the Nepalese princess gave my father the impetus he needed to break the Ratlam engagement, although he had already begun cooling off towards it after Maharaja Sajjan Singhji passed away. It was a sign of the changing times that my parents wanted me to meet the princess and decide whether I liked her or not. On our way back from Bombay to Jammu, therefore, we stopped off at Delhi and the meeting was arranged at Faridkot House over lunch. We were met by General and Rani Sarada and the princess who, although only a couple of months over twelve, was very pretty even at that age. We ate in silence while our parents—mainly the mothers—talked incessantly. After the meal we got into the car and I said 'yes'. The princess was, I learnt later, not even asked about her reactions. It was under these unlikely circumstances that our marriage was decided upon. Some people say that we have both been lucky, but I can speak only for myself.

We received a tumultuous reception when our chartered DC-3 touched down at Jammu. The whole town was out to greet us on my return from America after a prolonged absence, and the people of Jammu took the opportunity to reiterate their loyalty and affection for the Dogra ruling family. I had never seen so many people together at the same time; it took us the better part of three hours to get from the airport to the palace via the Raghunath Temple. In the days that followed I was whisked around to refugee camps where it was heart-rending to see the plight of thousands who had barely survived the tribal invasion. Many had lost all the members of their family in the gruesome massacres that took place in Muzaffarabad, Mirpur, Rajouri, Bhimbar and other towns. All had lost their homes and property, and were huddled together in a number of camps where they were totally dependent upon doles. My mother had done remarkable work in refugee relief, throwing herself heart and soul into the work, collecting money and spending many hundreds of thousands of rupees of her own. I went with her to most of the camps, and the refugees would fall at her feet with tears of gratitude. My father also came sometimes, but he was averse to displays of emotion and the visits with him had a rather more formal atmosphere.

A great deal had changed since I had left. The Indian Army

was now an important presence. My parents had excellent relations with senior army officers, and they would often come over in the evenings for a chat over drinks. The overall Army Commander for the J & K sector was General Kulwant Singh, while General Thimayya was the Divisional Commander in the Valley who had been responsible for the major counter-offensive that drove the invaders back until a ceasefire was declared under the United Nations auspices on 1 January 1949. There was also a distinct change in the sort of people who came to the palace. While in the past the visitors were confined to a small and carefully selected group of courtiers and advisers, now a large number of new faces were in and out, evidently part of a last, desperate attempt to win adherents in the political struggle against Sheikh Abdullah.

The burning issue at that time was the proposal for a plebiscite. While accepting the Instrument of Accession signed by my father, Lord Mountbatten as Governor-General of India had said in his reply:

In the special circumstances mentioned by Your Highness, my Government have decided to accept the accession of Kashmir State to the Dominion of India. Consistently with their policy that, in the case of any State where the issue of accession has been the subject of dispute, the question of accession should be decided in accordance with the wishes of the people of the State, it is my Government's wish that as soon as law and order have been restored in Kashmir and its soil cleared of the invaders, the question of the State's accession should be settled by a reference to the people.

This 'offer' became the main source of trouble and difficulty later, and Jawaharlal Nehru came in for a good deal of criticism for having unnecessarily internationalized the Kashmir dispute. Indeed, my father's earlier reluctance to accede to either dominion, and Jawaharlal's later offer of a plebiscite, are both matters upon which future historians will doubtless lavish generous criticism. And yet the trouble with historians is that they are seldom 'there', and therefore find it difficult to appreciate the intangible parallelogram of forces and factors at play at any given point in time and space. I have already had something to say about my father's dilemma. Jawaharlal also must have found himself in a difficult predicament. On the one hand was his deep attachment to Kashmir, the land of his forebears, and the compulsions of newly resurgent Indian nationalism. On the other was his genuine idealism, his total commitment to democracy, and his personal affection for Sheikh Abdullah. No doubt Sardar Patel would have handled the situation differently as, in fact, he did in Hyderabad and Junagadh. And yet when a nation has the fortune of a genuine visionary as its leader, it sometimes has to pay the price of idealism itself.

Plebiscite being the watchword at that time, this became the trump card in the hands of Sheikh Abdullah. As the man who was supposed to win the plebiscite for India, he could virtually demand his pound of flesh. And this he did repeatedly; not only by assuming power, but also by pursuing my father relentlessly. He made accusations against him for having organized the massacre of Muslims in Jammu through the RSS during the partition holocaust, accusations that have never been substantiated. We were told that he went to the extent of telling Jawaharlal that my father distributed sweets when Gandhiji was assassinated. Jawaharlal and my father were in any case hardly the best of friends, and Sheikh Abdullah was able to convince him that as long as my father remained in the State he could not possibly win the plebiscite. The political tension between them was becoming intolerable, and it was only a matter of time before one of them had to be eased out.

It will be useful here to recount some of the background of this conflict between two strong personalities—my father and Sheikh Abdullah. Even before the invasion, an effort had been made through my uncle Thakur Nachint Chand to arrange a meeting between them. Indeed, on 26 September 1947 Sheikh Abdullah had written to my father from jail a letter which Mehr Chand Mahajan described as a 'qualified apology'. It ran as follows:

May it Please Your Highness,

It is after about one and half year's incarceration that—as long wished—I had an opportunity of having detailed talks with Thakur Nachint Chand Ji. What unfortunate things happened during this period in the State I need not mention. But this is now realised by every well-wisher of the State that many of the regrettable happenings of the past have mainly been due to the misunderstandings which appear now to have deliberately been created by interested people in

6

order to achieve their own ends. R. B. Ramchandra Kak, the ex-Prime Minister through his mischievous methods and masterly man-oeuvrings brought these misunderstandings to a climax and succeeded in his attempt, though temporarily, to a certain extent. He painted me and my organization in the darkest colours and in everything that we did or attempted to do to bring Your Highness and your people closer; base and selfish motives were attributed to me. But God be thanked that all these enemies of Your Highness and the State stand exposed today.

In spite of what has happened in the past, I assure Your Highness that myself and my party have never harboured any sentiment of disloyalty towards Your Highness' person, throne or dynasty. The development of this beautiful country and the betterment of its people is our common aim and interest and I assure Your Highness the fullest and loyal support of myself and my organization. Not only this but I assure Your Highness, that any party, within or without the State which may attempt to create any impediments in our efforts to gain our goal, will be treated as our enemy and will be treated as such.

In order to achieve the common aim set forth above, mutual trust and confidence must be the mainstay. Without this it would not be possible to face successfully the great difficulties that beset our State on all sides at present.

Before I close this letter I beg to assure Your Highness once again of my steadfast loyalty and pray that God under Your Highness' aegis bring such an era of Peace, Prosperity and Good Government that it may be second to none and be an ideal for others to copy.

Your Highness' Most Obedient Subject
S. M. Abdullah

This hopeful letter led to Sheikh Abdullah's release from jail and was followed up by a meeting between him and my father at Gulab Bhavan at which, I was told, he even offered my father a gold sovereign in the traditional court manner. But evidently nothing concrete emerged, and soon the whole situation underwent a drastic change as a result of the Pakistani invasion and the accession. Thereafter the die was cast against my father, and the Sheikh rode the crest of a popular wave with the full support of Jawaharlal Nehru. Apart from his close personal friendship with the Sheikh, Jawaharlal was genuinely convinced that in the peculiar circumstances of Kashmir with its Muslim majority it was absolutely essential both for national and international reasons for Sheikh Abdullah to be fully involved in the government of the State. Thus in a letter to my father dated 13 November 1947 he wrote:

As I pointed out to you, the only person who can deliver the goods in Kashmir is Sheikh Abdullah. He is obviously the leading popular personality in Kashmir. The way he has risen to grapple with the crisis has shown the nature of the man. I have a high opinion of his integrity and his general balance of mind. He has striven hard and succeeded very largely in keeping communal peace. He may make any number of mistakes in minor matters, but I think he is likely to be right in regard to major decisions.

But the real point is that no satisfactory way out can be found in Kashmir except through Sheikh Abdullah. If that is so, full confidence must be placed in him. There is no half-way house between full confidence and a half and half affair which has little advantage and many disadvantages. Even if a risk has to be taken in giving this full confidence, that risk has to be taken. There is no other way as far as I can see it both from the short-term point of view and the long-term one. Sheikh Abdullah is earnestly desirous of co-operating and is amenable to any reasonable argument. I would suggest to you to keep in close personal touch with him and deal with him directly and not through intermediaries.

I have often wondered how very different the politics of the subcontinent would have been if some understanding could have been reached between the Sheikh and my father, both proud and authoritarian men. Looking through some of the papers that came to me after my father passed away, which includes the letter I have just quoted, it is clear that after power had been handed over to Sheikh Abdullah the tension between him and my father continued unabated. Evidently Jawaharlal did make an attempt to strike some sort of an equation with my father, as there are a number of long letters by him during the period 1947–8 in which he tried to make certain points about the prevalent political situation. But the tension between my father and the Sheikh came in the way of any real understanding developing. There were several causes of conflict. One was the future of the Jammu and Kashmir State Forces, of which my father remained Commander-in-Chief. Sheikh Abdullah evidently demanded that with his appointment as Prime Minister the administrative control of the State Forces should also be transferred to him. When this was strenuously objected to, he suggested that their operational and administrative control be handed over to the Indian Army. While operationally the forces had been under Indian Army control ever since the invasion, my father was evidently reluctant that their entity should be entirely merged with the Indian Army. In reply to a memorandum from Sheikh Abdullah he made two important points:

I have given careful thought to the suggestion made in the above memo. It appears that there are certain aspects of the question which have not probably struck you. I am, therefore, asking you to reconsider your opinion after giving your earnest consideration to the following:

(1) Firstly in case the administrative control of the State Army is transferred to the Union Government as suggested by you the Pakistan propagandists will make capital out of it and make a plausible case that the State has been completely annexed to Indian Union by taking over complete Military control. Such an impression should not be permitted to be created.

(2) Secondly the Pakistan suggestion that at the time of Plebiscite the Forces of Indian Union should be sent away may to some extent be forced on us. In case the administrative control of the State Forces is handed over it will be difficult for us to make out a case for the retention of the State Forces because administratively there will be no distinction between the two.

However, Sheikh Abdullah was adamant. In a long and angry letter to Jawaharlal Nehru he made a frontal attack upon the State Forces, accused them of all sorts of crimes and misdemeanours, and insisted that their separate entity should cease and that they should be entirely taken over by the Indian Army. To add to the pressure, he informed my father that his Government had decided to stop all the salaries and allowances of these troops with effect from 16 August 1948. The conflict continued for a long time, and it was only some years later that the merger with the Indian Army took place.

Another source of conflict were the 'Reserved Subjects' which were supposed to have been left under my father's authority, including pensions of various types to members of the ruling family, the hospitality (*Tawaza*) department, and so on. Then there was the question of land reforms. The Sheikh and his party were pressing for radical changes in the land tenancy system, while my father was obviously opposed to any such move. The Dharmarth Trust, a religious endowment created by the founder of the State, Maharaja Gulab Singh, which administered over a hundred Hindu temples and shrines in different parts of the State, also became a bone of contention. This Trust spent several lakhs of rupees on the feeding of refugees in Jammu after the invasion, but Sheikh Abdullah charged that Dharmarth money had been used for political purposes, although this allegation was never proved or substantiated, and was anxious that his Government should take over the Trust and its extensive assets. This matter became the subject of an intense and bitter controversy, and ultimately Sardar Patel had to personally intervene and a compromise was worked out whereby my father remained Sole Trustee, but a reputed firm of Chartered Accountants was appointed to undertake a thorough audit of the Trust funds.

Apart from the merits of these and other disputes, the basic fact was that my father and Sheikh Abdullah represented two political cultures so dissimilar and disparate that the possibility of any compromise was virtually non-existent. My father belonged to the feudal order and, with all his intelligence and ability, was not able to accept the new dispensation and swallow the populist policies of Sheikh Abdullah. The Sheikh, on the other hand, while a charismatic mass leader and a superb orator in Kashmiri, was imbued with a bitterly anti-Dogra and anti-monarchical attitude. His socio-economic policy spelt out several years earlier in a pamphlet entitled 'Naya Kashmir' was based on egalitarian and socialistic thinking in which the ruler, at best, would be a powerless figurehead.

Added to the ideological conflict between them was the complicating fact that the Sheikh really represented Kashmiri opinion which, although numerically in a majority, was confined to only one region of the State. My father, in turn, commanded the traditional loyalty of the Dogras who constituted a majority in the Jammu region. Thus the stark contradictions inherent in the multi-regional character of the Jammu and Kashmir State founded by my ancestors surfaced with the events that followed the British withdrawal in 1947. Superimposed upon this whole situation was the fact that the State had become the subject of an international dispute and for many years constituted a permanent item on the agenda of the United Nations, as a result of which the plebiscite offer hung constantly over our heads and constituted an additional element of tension and instability.

The hostility between my father and the Kashmiri leaders was greatly heightened by the fact that his move to Jammu on the night of 29 October 1947 in the wake of the tribal invasion (on the insistent advice of V. P. Menon) was seized upon by the Sheikh to attack and malign him in bitter and brutal fashion. It was presented to the country and the world that here was a cowardly ruler who fled his capital in the dead of night along with his family, jewels and courtiers, leaving his people to face the fury of the approaching onslaught. A barrage of vituperative propaganda was launched by the National Conference leaders, and was echoed by newspapers in Delhi and other parts of the country. The irony of the situation lay in the fact that Sheikh Abdullah himself had flown to Delhi on 25 October, two days before we left Srinagar, and did not return until after the Indian Army arrived. Even worse, my father was publicly accused by Sheikh Abdullah of having fomented communal riots in Jammu in which Muslims had been massacred, and for years he would say in his speeches that the hands of the Dogras were 'dyed in blood'. For a proud and highly sensitive man like my father, these attacks were naturally a source of great anguish and anger. It is to his abiding credit that, despite tremendous provocation, he maintained a dignified silence in public, and for the rest of his life said or did nothing that could have harmed the national interest at that critical juncture.

However, he did protest to Sheikh Abdullah in a memorandum dated 3 December 1948, as follows:

PRIME MINISTER

I would like to draw your attention to the malicious propaganda which is being carried on against my person inside the State and outside. I presume this has come to the notice of the Prime Minister and the Ministry but I find that no steps have been taken either to counteract or ban such activities. I am sending herewith some copies of extracts of the speeches of some of the Ministers and National Conference Leaders which also offend in the same manner.

I am sure you will agree that it is most improper both on constitutional and moral grounds for Ministers to indulge in this kind of propaganda. I put it to you that it should be as much the concern of my Government as of myself to ensure that the person of the Constitutional Head of the State, his dignity and position are fully respected and that any tendency to the contrary, from whatever quarter, is dealt with promptly and severely. I hope you will take suitable action immediately to counter these tendencies and this propaganda. I will be glad if you will let me know as soon as possible what you propose doing.

MAHARAJADHIRAJ
3.12.48

No reply is on file, but Sheikh Abdullah could hardly have been expected to respond favourably. Indeed, he redoubled his demand that my father should be forced to physically leave the State, by abdication or otherwise.

In the conflict of wills with my father, Sheikh Abdullah had a major advantage in the whole-hearted support of Jawaharlal Nehru. As against this my father was closely in touch with Sardar Patel, Minister for Home Affairs and the States Ministry, who often stood up for him against the constant harassment let loose by Sheikh Abdullah. The former Prime Minister of Jammu and Kashmir, Gopalaswami Ayyangar, was also in Jawaharlal's Cabinet, and because of his intimate knowledge of the State, his services were utilized on several occasions in dealing with Kashmir affairs. That this was deeply resented by the Sardar is evident from the correspondence published in the first volume of his letters, which reveals that at one stage this became so serious as to threaten a major rift between the two great leaders, and that the Sardar wrote out (but did not dispatch) his resignation on this very issue.

Ever since the accession, my father maintained close contact with Sardar Patel and wrote to him with regard to a number of important matters. The correspondence includes several appeals on behalf of my father against the constant harassment and humiliation directed at him by the Sheikh, and evidently the Sardar did intervene on several occasions to sort things out. But the main issue at the time was the Security Council deliberations, and the necessity of making drastic changes in the internal administration of the State could not be evaded. It seems that at first the 'Mysore model' was mooted, under which Sheikh Abdullah would be appointed Head of the Administration and my father would have a Dewan to look after the Reserved Subjects. Something on these lines was in fact attempted for a while, but riding a popular wave as he was, Sheikh Abdullah was clearly in no mood to accept anything short of a complete transfer of power. The correspondence also shows that my father was very unhappy with the slow progress of the military campaign against the raiders. This is clear from a long and passionate letter that he wrote to the Sardar on 31 January 1948. After a lengthy description of the unsatisfactory military situation, the never-ending influx of refugees and the deadlocked Security Council deliberations, he made some remarks which I quote at length because they reveal his state of mind at the time, and also contain the first hint of his possible withdrawal from the scene.

In the situation described above a feeling comes to my mind as to the possible steps that I may take to make so far as I am concerned a clean breast of the situation. Sometimes I feel that I should withdraw the Accession that I have made to the Indian Union. The Union only provisionally accepted the Accession and if the Union cannot recover back our territory and is going eventually to agree to the decision of the Security Council which may result in handing us over to Pakistan then there is no point in sticking to the Accession of the State to the Indian Union. For the time being it may be possible to have better terms from Pakistan but that is immaterial because eventually it would mean an end of the Dynasty and end of the Hindus and Sikhs in the State. There is an alternative possible for me and that is to withdraw the Accession and that may kill the reference to the UNO because Indian Union will have no right to continue the proceedings before the Council if the Accession is withdrawn. The result may be a return to the position the State held before the Accession. The difficulty in that situation however will be that the Indian Troops cannot be maintained in the State except as volunteers to help the State. I am prepared to take over command of my own Forces along with the Forces of the Indian Army as volunteers to help the State. I am prepared to lead my Army personally and to command, if the Indian Union agrees, also their troops. It would certainly hearten my people and the Troops. I know my country much better than any of your Generals will know it even during the next several months or years and I am prepared to take the venture boldly rather than merely keep on sitting here doing nothing. It is for you to consider whether the Indian Union will accept this in both the situations whether after the withdrawal of the Accession or even if the Accession continues. I am tired of my present life and it is much better to die fighting than watch helplessly the heart-breaking misery of my people.

So far as the internal political situation is concerned I have left the matter entirely to you personally. I am prepared to be constitutional Ruler of the State and when a new constitution is framed I am quite willing to give Responsible Government but I am not prepared to go beyond the Mysore Model because I am not satisfied that the leaders of the National Conference are for the time being very fit administrators or command the confidence of the Hindus and Sikhs and even of a large section of the Muslims. I must therefore keep certain reserved powers of which you are already aware and I must have a Dewan of my free choice as a member of the Cabinet and possibly as President.

Another alternative that strikes me is that if I can do nothing I should leave the State (short of abdication) and reside outside so that people do not think that I can do anything for them. For their grievance they can hold the Civil Administration responsible or the Indian Forces who are in charge of the Defence of the State. The responsibility will then clearly be either of the Indian Union or of the Administration of Sh. Abdulla. If there is any criticism those responsible can have it and the responsibility for the suffering of the people will not be mine. Of course I well anticipate that—as people started saying when I left Kashmir only on Mr Menon's advice that I had run away from Srinagar—they will say that I have left them in their hour of misery but it is no use remaining in a position where one can do nothing merely to avoid criticism. Of course if I go out of the State I will have to take the public into confidence and tell them the reasons why I am going out.

The Sardar's reply came on 9 February. The operative paragraph was short but categorical. He wrote:

I fully realize what an anxious time you must be having. I can assure you that I am no less anxious about the Kashmir situation and what [is] happening in the U.N.O., but whatever the present situation may be, a counsel of despair is entirely out of place.

Subsequent letters deal with the issue of a proclamation by my father handing over effective power to Sheikh Abdullah, the office and function of the Dewan Th. Baldev Singh Pathania, the definition and administration of the Reserved Subjects, the future of the J & K State Forces and, of course, Sheikh Abdullah's pronouncements. In a revealing letter to the Sardar dated 20 April 1948 my father wrote:

My dear Sardar Patel,

As I have mentioned to you and to Mr Menon and Mr Shankar also once or twice, there is one aspect of propaganda against me which has distressed me beyond words, particularly as it affects not only my position as a Ruler but my personal honour. I refer to the wild and baseless allegations that are being made against me that I left the Capital at the dead of night and removed truckloads of furniture and other belongings. I would ordinarily have dismissed these allegations but to my great regret and profound shock, they have found expression in some of the utterances of my present Prime Minister. I would invite your attention to the speech which Sh. Abdulla made before the Security Council in which he said the following words:

> 'The Maharaja in the dead of night left the Capital along with his courtiers and the result was absolute panic. There was no one to take over the control. This is the manner in which administration changed hands and we were de facto in charge of the administration. The Maharaja later on gave it a legal form.'

(2) How entirely divorced from facts this allegation is would, I am sure, be borne out by your Secretary Mr Menon at whose instance I reluctantly left Srinagar for Jammu. The other allegation that truckloads of belongings were removed is absolutely false and fantastic. The fact is that some lorries carrying the families of those officers who had already moved to Jammu on Government work and families of servants followed me. I felt morally responsible to afford transport facilities to these families. All my household effects which usually remain permanently at Srinagar have been and are still there. I am sure you will appreciate that such speeches and allegations when made by responsible and highly placed persons in the administration and by members of the National Conference are bound to create disaffection and promote feelings of estrangement between the Ruler and his people.

(3) You might ask why I am resuscitating this matter after so much lapse of time since the speech was made, but apart from the fact that those allegations are still being persisted in and are being given credence under continuous propaganda, the speech of my Prime Minister is being distributed in a pamphlet form headed 'Kashmir: Appeal to World Conscience'. I hope your Ministry will succeed in giving a lie to this propaganda by means of an authoritative pronouncement or communique explaining the correct facts and by persuading Sh. Abdulla to make amends for the lapse which he has made.

(4) While I am on this subject I should also like to refer to one important aspect of the propaganda which is being carried on against me on the lines that I was a despotic and autocratic ruler, that the popular

movement was directed against Dogra tyranny and that the present position has been reached as a result of fight put up by the people against me and my regime. Apart from the fact that I am prepared to maintain and establish to the satisfaction of any impartial person that at any given time, since 1934, the reforms which I gave to my people were in advance of those given by the Ruler of any State in India and that my attitude in relation to India's constitutional advancement has been much more progressive than that of any other Ruler I should like to ask whether any useful purpose could be served by raking up the past. For my part, I am endeavouring to forget all that was unpleasant in the past. Am I wrong in claiming a similar response from the persons in power in relation to me? Moreover, by presenting me as an unmitigated autocrat it is perhaps not realized that they merely help Pakistan propaganda. I should have thought that they would themselves realise the expediency of countering this propaganda of Pakistan rather than keep afresh old animosities, for, as some knowledgeable persons have told me, the justification of Poonch and Mirpur revolt can be sought in the pages of some of the publicity material issued by the Ministry.

(5) I hope that instructions from you to Sh. Abdulla on this point would go at least some way in repairing the damage done. I can assure you that had I not felt both these matters to have an important bearing from the propaganda point of view in order to win the State of Jammu & Kashmir for a permanent association with the Indian Dominion, I would not have laid so much stress on them.

Yours sincerely,
Hari Singh

It is clear, however, that even the Sardar was not in a position to restrain Sheikh Abdullah, and by the time I returned to India in February 1949 the situation had become quite impossible and a total deadlock reached. In March I turned eighteen, but the event passed off virtually unnoticed as the atmosphere was full of tension and foreboding. Soon thereafter my father received an invitation from Sardar Patel suggesting that he, my mother and I should visit Delhi for consultations. We left in April in a chartered DC-3. Little did I realize as we boarded the plane that only my father's ashes would ever return to his beloved Jammu.

Chapter 8

On our arrival in Delhi we stayed first at the Maidens Hotel in old Delhi and later shifted to the Imperial. Soon after we got there my father, my mother and I were invited by Jawaharlal Nehru to lunch with him at Teen Murti House. Indira Gandhi was hostess, and though my father and Jawaharlal were obviously uncomfortable in each other's presence, there was no open hostility. Evidently Jawaharlal had left it to the Sardar to get down to brass tacks with him. On 29 April we had a meal with the Sardar also, at which his daughter Maniben and his Private Secretary V. Shankar were present. After dinner my parents and the Sardar went into another room, and it was there that the blow fell. The Sardar told my father gently but firmly that although Sheikh Abdullah was pressing for his abdication, the Government of India felt that it would be sufficient if he and my mother absented themselves from the State for a few months. This, he said, was in the national interest in view of the complications arising from the plebiscite proposal then being actively pursued in the United Nations. He added that as I had now returned from America, I should be appointed Regent by my father to carry out his duties and responsibilities during his absence.

My father was stunned. Although rumours to the effect that he might be pushed out of the State had been in the air for some time, he never believed that even the Sardar would advise him to adopt this course. He emerged from the meeting ashen-faced, while my mother was fighting desperately to keep back her tears. The Sardar also looked grim as he saw us to the door. I realized at once that something was seriously wrong, but didn't dare ask what the matter was. We drove back to the hotel in dead silence. My father immediately got into a huddle with his advisers, Bakshi Tek Chand and Mehr Chand Mahajan, and his staff officers. My mother went to her room where she flung herself on her bed and burst into tears. I followed her there, and when she had calmed down a bit she told me that she and my father were being pushed out of the State and that the Government of India wanted me to be appointed Regent.

It was at this critical juncture that Jawaharlal invited me to the first of several breakfasts at his residence. I can still recall my excitement as I walked up the steps of Teen Murti House to the dining-room. The table was set for two, Indira Gandhi and the boys having already finished their meal. Jawaharlal walked in briskly, shook hands with a friendly 'Hello, Tiger', and we sat down to breakfast. Over the meal, which lasted almost an hour, Jawaharlal asked me a few general questions and then settled down into a long monologue. In his chaste accent he spoke of the fact that a new India was being created, that the old feudal order was rapidly collapsing and that as a young man I should readily adjust myself to the new situation. He then went on to outline the Kashmir problem, the role of Sheikh Abdullah and the importance in the national interest of establishing a harmonious situation in the State. He said briefly that my father was evidently unable or unwilling to accept the new dispensation, and that both he and Sheikh Abdullah were of the view that I should be appointed Regent so as to solve the present deadlock. When he spoke of the future of India his eyes glowed with a gentle fire and his voice took on a ringing note.

I had admired this man ever since I was a schoolboy, and it was a fascinating experience to be near him and to listen to him. When he talked of the vast, historic forces that were sweeping across the world it was as if the *Discovery of India* was coming alive before my eyes. How different this was from the constricted viewpoints that I heard in my father's circle and the all-pervasive atmosphere of tension and intrigue at home. In my school days I had dreamed of becoming a perfect ruler, of doing something substantial for the people. I now realized that rulership had gone, never to return, but here was an even more exciting opportunity of doing something in the broader national interest, and at the personal behest of one of the greatest leaders of our times.

For the next few days the tension steadily mounted. We had moved into the Imperial Hotel where we occupied several suites, and there was a constant stream of people coming in to see my father. Prominent among them was V. Shankar who, with the Sardar's health steadily deteriorating, was becoming increasingly important in the States Ministry. Sardar Patel called me over one evening and had a long, friendly talk about the whole situation. While Jawaharlal's conversation was in the broader context of Indian nationalism, the Sardar chose a narrower canvas. He said that while he fully realized and admitted that an injustice was being done to my father, he had to agree to this in the broader national interest mainly due to Sheikh Abdullah's insistence. He also said that I should face the situation bravely and undertake my new responsibilities with courage and confidence. His talk was a source of great encouragement to me at that difficult juncture. Soon thereafter the Sardar left for Dehra Dun, and it was decided that my parents and I would also go there later to visit him. Meanwhile, my father was grappling with the virtual ultimatum served upon him by the Government of India, and was gradually coming round to accepting the inevitability of leaving the State. There was some pressure upon me to decline the Regentship, but I indicated as gently as I could that I did not think it would be appropriate for the whole family to leave the State, thus severing all ties with Jammu and Kashmir.

I had barely turned eighteen, but due perhaps to the unusual circumstances in which I had grown up I discovered that I was quite capable of holding my own in discussions even with very senior leaders. While I showed no outer signs of lack of self-confidence, inwardly, I must admit, I was often on the verge of panic. The last few years had been so full of change, and my own prolonged absence in America had also contributed towards creating a strange and unsettling atmosphere. All the familiar landmarks of my childhood had disappeared, and even my mother, with whom I had such close emotional links, seemed to be on the verge of psychological collapse. In fact, her position was excruciatingly difficult; on the one hand was her loyalty to my father despite their temperamental differences, and on the other was her devotion to her only child. Characteristically, my father never discussed the problem with me directly. The dialogue would take place either through his Private Secretary, Pandit Bhimsen Mahey, or Mehr Chand Mahajan, who remained his close confidant even after relinquishing the Prime Ministership. It seems that after the initial shock my father reconciled himself to leaving the State for a while, although I think he realized that it would not be easy for him ever to return. He was, however, totally opposed to abdication, and reiterated this in a letter written to Sardar Patel on 6 May. I reproduce below the full text of his letter and of the reply that the Sardar sent from Dehra Dun, because they have a vital bearing on subsequent developments in my life.

My dear Sardar Patelji,

With reference to the discussions I had with you on 29th April and 1st May 1949 I have been revolving the matter in my mind and am now in a position to let you have my settled reactions to the proposal in regard to my temporary absence from the State which you put to me.

I should like to say at the outset that I was completely taken aback by this proposal but coming as it did from you, in whom I have since the very beginning placed implicit trust and confidence and whose advice I have throughout followed on the many questions affecting me personally and my State both in the present and in future, I have been able somehow to adjust myself to it. I would not, however, be human if I did not express my sense of keen disappointment and bewilderment at having been called upon to make such a sacrifice of prestige, honour and position when all along I have been content to follow, sometimes even against my own judgment and conscience, the advice in regard to the constitutional position in the State which I have been receiving from the Prime Minister of India or yourself, sometimes even against arrangements which were agreed to only a few months before. Nor would it be fair on my part to conceal from you my own feeling that while Sheikh Abdullah has been allowed to depart from time to time as suited his inclinations from the pledged and written word, to act consistently in breach of the loyalty which he professed to me prior to his release from Jail and the oath of allegiance which he took when he assumed office, and to indulge openly along with his colleagues in a campaign of vilification and foul calumny against me, both inside the State and outside, I should have had to be driven from position to position—each of which I thought I held on the advice of the States Ministry.

The contrast naturally fills me with poignant feelings. However, once again putting my complete trust in your judgment and benevolent intentions towards us, I might be prepared to fall in with your wishes and to absent myself from the State for a period of three or four months in consideration of the fact as emphasized by you namely complications created by the reference to U.N.O. and the plebiscite issue.

There are, however, certain questions arising out of this proposal on which I would venture to make my position clear to you and on which

I would be grateful to have your assurance. I hope you will kindly appreciate the necessity of my seeking these assurances. I have to think of the immediate future in the light of my bitter experience of the last several months and I owe it to myself, my family and my dynasty to procure a clear declaration in respect of these matters.

1. I should like to be assured that this step is not a prelude to any idea of abdication. I should like to make it clear now that I cannot entertain the latter idea even for a moment and am fully prepared to take the consequences. I regard such a demand from my Prime Minister and his colleagues as a clear breach of the many understandings on which constitutional arrangements have been based from time to time and a positive net of his disloyalty, treachery and deception.

2. Sheikh Abdullah should be clearly told to stop the campaign of vilification against me and to abandon all activities, both on his part and that of his followers, aimed at securing my abdication. I feel that the sacrifice which I am being called upon to make would be in vain if I continued to be the target of their public or private attacks.

3. There should be a clear assurance of protection of myself and my adherents against any victimization. In this connection I should like especially to draw your attention to the facts that have been reported to me about persons having been detained in jail for their failure to sign for my abdication.

4. The question that I should remain out of the State for three or four months for reasons of health, will, I am afraid, not be believed by anybody and is likely to give rise to many misgivings and speculations within and outside the State as

(*i*) everybody knows that I am not in such a state of health as would necessitate a long rest outside the State. I have, on your advice, been recently touring parts of the Jammu Province in the heat of April.

(*ii*) For everybody in bad health Kashmir is considered to be the best health resort and it will certainly look strange if I went outside the State giving out that I am doing so for reasons of health.

(*iii*) Wherever I take my temporary residence I cannot confine myself to the four walls of the house. I am bound to meet people, who, when they meet me, will never believe that I am staying there for reasons of health.

(*iv*) Some other reason which may be plausible and may also at the same time not compromise my dignity and position, should be given out. The best thing would be that the Government of India should find a suitable position for me in Delhi where my services may be utilized in a fitting manner during the above period of 3 or 4 months.

5. It is a matter of paramount necessity that Her Highness should remain with the Yuvaraj in the State during the period of my absence.

He is young and impressionable and requires paternal guidance and personal supervision of at least one of the parents. I can see no reason either of political expediency or justice in insisting on the separation of a mother from her only child whom she is seeing after thirteen months of absence abroad. Considerations of humanity alone should suffice to rule out this altogether.

6. My Private Estates, Houses and other property should be protected against the aggressive acts of Sheikh Abdullah's party. They will attempt to take possession of my Houses, Gardens, Lands and other property. The Indian Dominion should guarantee against that act of aggression. While I am there they dare not do these things but in my absence they will attempt this. I have received information that even during the last few days, after I left Jammu for Delhi, encroachments have been made on my lands at Srinagar.

7. No change should be made without my consent in the present arrangements regarding the State Forces or the constitutional position, Prerogatives etc. of the Ruler as now subsisting. Arrangements will continue for me to draw my Staff (both State and Private Deptts) from amongst Officers of my Forces. Guards mounted by my Forces at my Palaces will also continue as at present as per agreement reached vide my letter of 30th August and Mr Menon's reply of 3rd September thereto. I shall also take whatever staff etc. I require with me outside.

8. I should be entitled during my stay in India to suitable strength of military guards wherever I stay.

9. Yuvaraj's safety and protection should be the concern of the Indian Dominion. State and Indian Military should guard his person.

10. Outstanding matters with the State Military, Civil Lists, Hazur Departments etc. should be decided with me immediately.

In conclusion I wish to say that I shall take the final decision on getting assurances from you on the points above mentioned.

With kindest regards,

Imperial Hotel,
New Delhi.
6th May, 1949.

Yours very sincerely,
Hari Singh

After about a fortnight, Sardar Patel's reply came from Dehra Dun.

Camp: Doon Court,
Dehra Dun.
23rd May 1949

My dear Maharaja Sahib,

Thank you for your letter dated the 6th May 1949.

2. I am very glad to know that Your Highness has reconciled

7

yourself to the proposal which I put forward at my discussion with you. It was with no light heart that I did so. No one can be more cognizant than myself of the attitude which Your Highness has adopted ever since you signed the Instrument of Accession. I am grateful to Your Highness for the spirit of co-operation and understanding which you have always extended to me and also for the kind sentiments which you have expressed. I can assure Your Highness that, before putting forward my proposal, I had, after careful consideration, come to the conclusion that the interests alike of Your Highness, the dynasty and the country demanded the step which you have now agreed to take. I know full well the personal sacrifice involved in it, but, I am sure, along with so many other changes to which Your Highness has accustomed yourself, you will undertake this step also with a sense of duty to your country and in a spirit of calm resignation to the superior dictates of events.

3. Regarding the points which Your Highness has referred to me, I should like to state that the question of Your Highness' abdication does not arise. We have made the position quite plain to Sheikh Mohammad Abdulla, and we hope there will be an end to the public controversies centering round this matter as well as to the derogatory references to Your Highness in the press and on the platform in the State. Your Highness will, of course, appreciate that the future constitution of the State would be determined by the duly elected constituent assembly. I am afraid, in the absence of any specific instances of victimization to which Your Highness refers in paragraph 4, it may not be possible for me to give any assurance, but I can tell Your Highness that, if any such instances are brought to our notice, we shall look into them and try to see that justice is done.

4. I appreciate what Your Highness says in regard to the reasons for your remaining outside the State, but I feel that it would be best just to say that Your Highness has decided, after the strain of the last so many months and continued ill-health, to stay out of the State for a few months. The actual period need not be stated.

5. We have carefully considered the question of Her Highness staying with the Yuvaraja during your absence, but for a variety of reasons, we feel that it would be best, for the present, for her also to stay away for a while. Later, she can certainly visit the Yuvaraja from time to time, and the Yuvaraja can also visit Your Highness and Her Highness occasionally.

6. We would be grateful if Your Highness would let me have a list of the private estates, houses and other property belonging to Your Highness and referred to in para 6 of your letter. On receipt of the list we shall take up the matter with your Ministry. In the meantime, I hope that, with the understanding that has been reached with Sheikh

Mohammad Abdulla on the various controversial issues, he will himself take steps to safeguard Your Highness' property against encroachments. In particular, I hope that the feelings which he entertains for the Yuvaraja will succeed in closing the chapter of the past several months and in introducing a healthy change in the approach of both the Government and the National Conference workers to these and other problems affecting Your Highness and the family personally and the dynasty in general. I hope that no need for a change in the arrangements to which Your Highness has referred in paragraph 7 would arise, but should any such need arise, we would of course consult Your Highness. We would also make necessary arrangements for guarding you during your stay in India, and we take full responsibility for the Yuvaraja's safety and protection.

7. As regards outstanding matters, we have already informed Your Highness separately that your Civil List has been fixed at Rs. 15 lakhs, out of which Rs. 6 lakhs would be paid by the State and Rs. 9 lakhs by the Government of India during the period of the emergency. Out of this sum, Your Highness will have to make allotment to Her Highness and the Yuvaraja. The latter's expenses would, of course, be larger than before on account of his being Regent. I hope Your Highness will agree to make a suitable allowance for him, bearing in mind his needs. I should be glad to know your suggestion in this respect. Similarly, I should welcome Your Highness' proposal regarding Her Highness' allowance. As regards Hazur Departments, Sheikh Sahib has already agreed to our suggestion that an allowance of Rs. 5 lakhs should be made to Your Highness for this purpose. A list of items, which will be controlled by Your Highness, and during your absence, by the Yuvaraja as Regent, has been furnished to Sheikh Sahib, and he has promised to let us have his comments as soon as possible. After his comments are received, we shall finalise the whole matter, but in the meantime, Your Highness can make suitable allocation to major and other heads of the expenditure on State Departments from out of the allotment of Rs. 5 lakhs.

With kindest regards,

Yours sincerely,
Vallabhbhai Patel

The same day, Sardar Patel sent a copy of this letter to Jawaharlal Nehru. The covering note contains the following paragraph: 'As regards the Yuvaraj, we have had a very detailed talk with him and I have impressed upon him the significance and importance of the agreements reached and the consequences which flow therefrom. He is a sensible lad and I think he appreciated the situation fairly well and realizes his responsibilities. He is, of course, still in his teens and would require some guidance. I am looking out for a suitable adviser for him on whose advice he can lean. We shall have to be very careful in the choice of a suitable person.'

Soon after this correspondence took place, all of us went up to Dehra Dun at the suggestion of Sardar Patel who was himself convalescing there. My parents stayed in a hotel, but at the Sardar's special invitation I was his guest for three weeks in the famous Circuit House known as Doon Court, set in an extensive estate with lovely flowers, trees and shrubs. Evidently he and Jawaharlal had decided that it would be useful for me to stay with him for a while before taking up my new responsibilities. The Sardar was at that time in very poor health, and his daughter Maniben was constantly ministering to him with great devotion. He ate mainly in his own room, but would sometimes call me and talk about Kashmir. While he did not have the fire and fervour of the Prime Minister, he spoke with a quiet confidence that was very impressive. Here was a man, one felt, for whom no problem was too formidable to tackle. It was only about Kashmir, which Jawaharlal was handling himself, that the Sardar was obviously unhappy. Although he never criticized Jawaharlal in my presence, it was clear from his conversation that he did not approve of his special relationship with Sheikh Abdullah, whom he evidently distrusted and disliked.

While at Dehra Dun I was able to revisit the Doon School for the first time since leaving it three years earlier. By now I was walking without the aid of a cane, although I would carry a limp for the rest of my life. It was curious coming back to school and seeing again the rooms and grounds where I had spent so many years as a boy. Mr Foot had returned to England and J. A. K. Martyn was Headmaster. Jack Gibson, still Housemaster of Kashmir House, greeted me like a long lost friend and we played several games of chess at his cottage. I also went up to Mussoorie for a weekend which we spent largely with Lakshmi Nivas Birla and his family who were close to the Sardar and V. Shankar.

My parents returned to Delhi earlier, and by the time I got back it had been decided that my father would appoint me Regent and that I would fly up to Srinagar on 20 June to take up my new responsibilities. I learnt that my mother had also agreed, very reluctantly, to leave the State but that, as she could not take the heat of Bombay, she would go to Kasauli instead. One thing remained to be done before I went up to Srinagar. A devout Hindu, my mother insisted that my sacred thread ceremony should be performed. This was done at 5 Hastings Road, where Mehr Chand Mahajan lived. The Pandits came down from Jammu, and two young Rajput servants of my father went through the ceremony along with me. We all got into dhoties, but, despite the Raj Pandit's insistence, my voluble protests saved my head from being shaved as is traditionally done on this occasion. Instead, a symbolic tuft of hair was cut off, saving me from the fate of having to assume the Regency of Jammu and Kashmir looking like a monk.

On the night of 19 June I could hardly sleep. My mind was a welter of conflicting emotions and thoughts. I was obviously embarking on a delicate assignment fraught with risk and even danger. My father made no secret of his unhappiness at the whole situation, and although he had bowed to the inevitable I realized that our relationship had been soured in the process. My mother also was breaking away on her own, which added a new element of emotional instability to the entire situation. I had no one to rely on except Jawaharlal's support and such inner resources as I could summon at that critical juncture. 20 June 1949 was an important landmark in my life. My father, his staff and servants left by train early in the morning for Bombay. My mother, uncle and her maidservants left by car for Kasauli soon after. For half an hour I sat absolutely alone in my hotel room, poised between the weight of the past and the burdens of the future. It was one of those critical moments in life that remains for ever embedded in one's memory. With a considerable effort I pulled myself together and walked out of the hotel accompanied by my staff officer, Captain Mahel Singh. We drove to Safdarjung airport where a DC-3 was waiting to fly me to Srinagar along with Vishnu Sahay, Secretary for Kashmir Affairs, a senior I.C.S. officer who had been deputed by the Prime Minister to accompany me.

The proclamation that my father had signed on that very morning, before he left, was short and cryptic. It read as follows:

PROCLAMATION

Whereas I have decided for reasons of health to leave the State for a temporary period and to entrust to the Yuvaraj Shri Karansinghji Bahadur for that period all my powers and functions in regard to the Government of the State.

Now, therefore, I hereby direct and declare that all powers and functions, whether legislative, executive, or judicial which are exercisable by me in relation to the State and its Government, including in particular my right and prerogative of making laws, of issuing Proclamations, Orders and of pardoning offenders, shall during the period of my absence from the State be exercisable by the Yuvaraj Shri Karansinghji Bahadur.

Hari Singh
MAHARAJADHIRAJ

As the plane took off it struck me that two critical events in my life had been associated with an air flight. I remembered flying off to America as an invalid, and then returning to the curiously muted welcome in India. Once again I was flying off, almost literally into the unknown. Of course, the valley was well known to me, but I realized that the Kashmir I was now going to was substantially different from the one I had known thus far. Although I was going as Head of State, it was virtually on sufferance of Sheikh Abdullah who wielded effective power. In one of his petulant moods my father had said over lunch, much to my mother's irritation, that even if I went as Regent I would be unceremoniously thrown out in disgrace by Sheikh Abdullah within a few months. Though I shared my mother's resentment at this grim prophecy, I could not easily dismiss it when I considered the political developments over the last few years.

We were scheduled to fly direct to Srinagar, but due to bad weather and the primitive aviation aids at that time, we had to land in Jammu and stay there for an hour before proceeding. When the plane took off from Jammu we were engulfed in thick cloud. It was only as we crossed the Banihal Pass that the clouds broke and the valley of Kashmir lay before us, glittering in all its indescribable beauty like some rare jewel nestling in the heart of the mighty Himalaya.

Chapter 9

At the Srinagar airport Sheikh Abdullah and his entire Cabinet, along with senior officials, had gathered to greet me. The Sheikh met me at the top of the steps and then introduced me to his colleagues. At that time there were nine Cabinet Ministers, important among whom were the Deputy Prime Minister, Bakshi Ghulam Mohammad, the main organizer in the Sheikh's party, and Mirza Mohammed Afzal Beg, the wily Revenue Minister who had been in the Government even under my father during a short-lived experiment in self-rule a few years earlier. Ghulam Mohammed Sadiq, Girdhari Lal Dogra, Sham Lal Saraf, Colonel Pir Mohammad and Sardar Budh Singh were also in the Cabinet, while the bearded Maulana Masoodi was General Secretary of the National Conference.

After the welcome we all drove up to Karan Mahal. It was exciting coming back after so many years in vastly different circumstances to the house where I had spent much of my childhood. I still remember the mingled feelings of exhilaration and apprehension as I alighted from the car and entered the lovely villa, its garden ablaze with flowers and a cool breeze coming in from across the lake. It had been miserably hot in Delhi, and merely getting away from the heat was a great relief. Vishnu Sahay, who was functioning as part-time Adviser, stayed in the guest cottage across the road, and spent a fortnight in Srinagar before returning to Delhi. He was an able man, unflappable and shrewd in his observations, and in the early days of my Regency was a help to me in putting things in their proper perspective without any emotionalism or fanfare.

Although I savoured my newly acquired independence, I fully realized that I was actually in a rather difficult position. Sheikh Abdullah was the outstanding personality on the scene, and Jawaharlal Nehru had specifically asked me to work in harmony with him. Physically an impressive man, the Sheikh was at that time at the height of his powers. He would come over from time to time and give me long lectures on the political situation. He never mentioned my father directly, and I

found that he displayed some genuine friendliness towards me.
I was aware, though, that my position was a precarious one and
that in a way I was on a trial run. My father was not really
happy at my having become Regent, and there was a certain
sullen disapproval from the Dogra public in Jammu. In all my
actions, therefore, I had to try and steer a middle path between
appearing subservient to the Sheikh on the one hand and
offending him and Jawaharlal on the other.

Meanwhile there was a lot of interesting work to be done.
The Kashmir issue being very much in the fore at the United
Nations, a great deal of significance was attached to the U.N.
observers and representatives who were in Srinagar at that time,
headed by a Frenchman, General Delvoi. The group was drawn
from various European and South American countries, and
several had brought their families with them. There were
parties at various places, including the residence of the dashing
and witty Divisional Commander, General T. S. Thimaiyya and
his wife Nina. 'Timmy' was great fun, and exuded charm and
charisma. He was adored by his troops and was also very
popular with the civilian administration. Soon after I got up to
Srinagar I went with him to some of the forward areas on the
Ceasefire Line. We crossed the 10,000 foot Nashtachoor Pass
and visited Tangdhar and Tithwal. It was my first exposure to
the greater Himalayas beyond the Kashmir valley, and an
unforgettable experience. Looking at the mountains from my
Srinagar house was one thing; being in them was quite a
different sensation. The air was crisp, and the wind swished
continuously through the great deodar trees which covered
large areas.

Timmy was in high spirits, driving our jeep himself and
regaling us with graphic details of the battles fought to free
these areas from the invaders only a year ago. The troops were
in fine fettle and seemed genuinely pleased to see us. It was the
first of numerous encounters I have had with Indian Army
personnel living under the most difficult conditions, and I have
never failed to be impressed by their devotion to duty and their
uncanny capacity to adapt to the environment. The cordiality
between the army and the civilian population was also impressive. Once across the Pass, the people were Panjabi- not
Kashmiri-speaking, but despite their close physical and ethnic

proximity to Pakistan-occupied territory I saw no trace of hostility or resentment. In fact, I was probably the first member of the Dogra ruling family to visit those areas, and they greeted me with great affection. Later we did a similar trip across the Zojila Pass where, in a historic manoeuvre often compared to Hannibal's crossing of the Alps with his elephants, Timmy had taken tanks for the first time in human history to such heights and had routed the startled invaders. On the other side of Zojila we stayed for a night at the small village of Dras, believed to be one of the coldest inhabited places in the world.

In addition to others, I met at this stage a person who was to play a significant role in my political life, Durga Prasad Dhar. Handsome, smooth and brilliant, 'D.P.' was the scion of one of the most distinguished Kashmiri Pandit families in the valley, but very early he had become actively associated with the National Conference. Although only a Deputy Minister, he was widely accepted as being the real brain behind Sheikh Abdullah's regime. He was excellent at army–civil liaison, and acted as a valuable link between the State Government and the Government of India. He had a remarkable mind which, however, he turned generally to brilliant manoeuvring rather than solid achievement. He was younger than the other Ministers, and we got on well together. This friendship was to pay useful dividends in the crisis that lay only four years ahead.

Jawaharlal made two visits to Srinagar during the summer of 1949, and I went to Delhi twice and stayed with him at Teen Murti House. He was a charming host, and despite his crushing schedule always found time to inquire after his guests. We would usually meet over meals, and it was here that I first met Pandit Govind Ballabh Pant, a large man with a walrus moustache and a shaking head that belied his sharp and shrewd mind, and the wiry, mephistophelian Krishna Menon. Padmaja Naidu was also living in the house, exuding good humour and *joie de vivre* despite her constant ill health. Many years later after Jawaharlal had passed away, she became a close friend and we discovered that she was an unusually warm and affectionate human being. As far as Jawaharlal was concerned, his physical and mental agility always impressed me. When he entered a room it was as though a breath of energy had blown in. He moved with a springy gait, as if ready at any moment to break into a run. And yet when he settled back on a sofa to talk his face would go thoughtful, and a strange sadness would cover his handsome features. He spoke beautifully, elocuting each word in a soft, civilized accent. But it was his smile that was the most memorable—pensive and strangely appealing.

During that summer in the valley I revisited many of my childhood haunts, specially Dachigam and Thricker. I did some shooting and fishing, and hosted endless lunch and tea parties for visiting dignitaries and local luminaries. I had just turned eighteen but was full of confidence and subdued excitement at being on my own for the first time. I visited a number of the famous Hindu shrines in the valley, which my father seldom, if ever, went to. His approach to religion had been largely formal, but taking after my mother I regularly performed some puja every morning before going into circulation, and also developed an interest in temples and shrines.

One incident occurred which preshadowed the tensions that lay ahead. The annual festival at the famous shrine dedicated to the Goddess Khir Bhawani fell on a certain auspicious day in June. The Kashmiri Pandits led by Pandit Parmanand, an able officer of great integrity who had just retired as Accountant General, were keen that I should visit the shrine on that occasion. It was clear that despite Sheikh Abdullah's secular protestations the tiny Pandit minority was not feeling very happy under the new dispensation. I readily agreed to go, and my visit was announced. Soon thereafter I got a message from Sheikh Abdullah saying that it was better if I did not go on that day. This placed me in an awkward dilemma, but having given them a commitment I felt I could not let the Pandits down. I received a tumultuous reception at the shrine where thousands had assembled. Elderly ladies embraced me and kissed me on the forehead, a gesture reserved only for those very dear to them. It took me almost three hours to complete the puja around the sacred pool, in which the water mysteriously changes from time to time. It is believed that the colour presages future events, and that dark colours are an ill omen. It is a curious fact that for months before the Pakistani invasion the water had turned pitch black, and also that, though the shrine remained for many months in the area under the occupation of the invaders who destroyed all other Hindu, Sikh and Christian places of worship, not a leaf in Khir Bhawani was touched. Throughout my presence at the shrine the air was rent with greeting slogans, including some of *Dogra Raj Zindabad*. Although the Sheikh never mentioned the matter to me, I learnt that he was very upset that I went there. How could the Lion of Kashmir tolerate any rival, even though he was yet only a tiger cub?

To Pandit Parmanand also I owe a deep debt of gratitude for having introduced me to Sanskrit. I had never studied a word of that magnificent language either at school or college. It was Pandit Parmanand who urged and insisted that I should begin learning Sanskrit, and he would come over to my house thrice a week to teach me some simple verses. Thus it was that, as in the case of English, I learnt Sanskrit not through grammar but directly by ear, and soon found that I could remember and recite passages by heart without undue difficulty. The key lay in the superb musical and metrical quality of Sanskrit verse, whether it is the liturgical majesty of the Vedas, the glowing wisdom of the Upanishads, the immortal teachings of the Bhagavad Gita or the superb hymns of Adi Shankaracharya.

Another development at this point had an important impact on my future life. Soon after I got up to Srinagar I thought it might be a good idea to renew my contacts with the academic world. I asked the Director of Education to suggest the name of a scholar who could visit me regularly to discuss current economic and political problems. He sent a Professor P. N. Chaku, with whom I immediately struck up a valuable rapport. Professor Chaku was an accomplished intellectual and introduced me to a number of important political and economic concepts, including the ideas of Keynes in the field of economics, Laski in political science and Marx in the context of a developing economy. I discovered again a genuine interest in the world of ideas, and began reading extensively. At that time Bertrand Russell and Aldous Huxley were the two authors who influenced me most. Russell's translucent prose and Huxley's imaginative formulations had a deep impact upon me. I still have a letter each from these great writers in response to my 'fan' letters, and despite disagreement in some matters my respect for them remains intact.

In my capacity as Regent I replaced my father as titular

Commander-in-Chief of the Jammu and Kashmir State Forces. By that time these troops had for all practical purposes become part of the Indian Army, and yet unlike the numerous other forces of Indian States that had acceded to the Indian Union, ours had not been formally merged and still retained their separate entity. In effect, of course, the office of Commander-in-Chief was a purely formal one and involved only signing a few papers from time to time. Also formal, but closer to my own interests, was the office of Chancellor of the newly formed Jammu and Kashmir University that I assumed ex-officio as Head of the State. Before 1947 educational institutions in the State had been affiliated to Panjab University based in Lahore, but after Partition the need for a separate university in the State was urgently felt. This was set up through an Ordinance issued by my father in 1948, as there was no legislature in the State at that time. The first formal convocation of the new University was held in Srinagar on 24 September 1949 over which, as Chancellor, I presided. Jawaharlal came up to Srinagar for the occasion. I had sent him an advance copy of my speech and in a letter of 11 September he wrote to me: 'Sheikh Saheb arrived here this evening and gave me a copy of the speech you intend delivering as Chancellor of the University. I have just glanced through it and I find it very interesting. Surely you must be by far the youngest Chancellor that a University has had.'

The convocation itself was a colourful affair. We all wore black gowns and pink turbans, and entered the enclosure in solemn procession. Sheikh Abdullah was Pro-Chancellor, so he, Jawaharlal and I walked together. After giving away degrees and prizes, I read out my speech and then requested Jawaharlal to address the gathering. I started then on a principle that I have consistently followed of writing my own speeches. The only exceptions, of course, were the Addresses to the Legislature which I had to deliver every year, but even for those I would ask for a draft and then try and put the material into my own words. Evidently my speech that day was well received, as I was widely congratulated by all present after the event, but perhaps this was only because of the novelty of having a teenage Chancellor.

In the afternoon we were all taken out in a boat procession on the Jhelum. I remember having sat with my father on one of these processions many years earlier, where brocade covered barges were rowed upstream by dozens of well-trained Kashmiri boatmen wearing white uniforms and yellow turbans. The boats and the boatmen were still there, but now a decade later the whole context had drastically changed. Jawaharlal, Sheikh Abdullah and I sat in the main barge, while other members of Nehru's party, including Gopalaswami Ayyangar, Sardar Baldev Singh, Rajkumari Amrit Kaur and N. V. Gadgil (all members of his Cabinet), as well as the Commander-in-Chief of the Indian Army General Cariappa followed in smaller boats. The banks of the Jhelum were crowded with the people of Srinagar who turned out in tens of thousands to greet Jawaharlal. As we passed under each of the historic seven bridges it seemed as if they would collapse under the sheer weight of people waving greeting flags and chanting slogans. School children in their thousands, smartly turned out in their uniforms, added to the life and colour of the whole scene. It was a dramatic and memorable event for me, and I felt proud to be with a national leader of Jawaharlal's stature under those circumstances. It was also an impressive show of political strength on the part of Sheikh Abdullah and his National Conference, and belied the vicious propaganda relentlessly indulged in by Pakistan to the effect that the Kashmiris were groaning under the military occupation of Indian troops. Anyone who witnessed that procession—and there were a number of foreign newsmen and camera teams present—could not have failed to be impressed by the genuine outpouring of love, affection and hope that Jawaharlal evoked at that historic juncture.

The Kashmir season was now drawing to a close, and we began making plans to go down to Jammu for the annual 'darbar move'. Then, as now, the State Government was based for the six summer months (May through October) in the summer capital, Srinagar, and for the other six months in the winter capital, Jammu. This is a political imperative, because in the State of Jammu *and* Kashmir both major regions have to be given equal importance. Indeed, it was in the inability to hold the scales even between the two regions that the seeds of much future tension and conflict are to be found. I decided that we would move down on 7 November, but before that I thought

I would get in some more fishing and shooting which improves as the autumn advances towards winter. I had even begun playing some tennis despite my stiff hip. My plan was to stay in Jammu for a few weeks and then call on my father in Bombay. He had heard from the Nepal Ranas, and my wedding had been fixed for 15 January next year. Everything seemed to be getting along smoothly.

On 29 October a Chakor shoot had been arranged at Khrew, a few miles out of Srinagar. We set off in the morning; I sat in the front seat along with the driver, while Brigadier Rawat, Captain Mahel Singh, my ADC, and my black labrador retriever, Dusky, got in behind. It had rained the previous night, and except for the tarred portion the roads were slippery. We had hardly driven five minutes when, just past the ancient Pandrethan temple, a truck moved onto the rough in order to give way to our car. Suddenly, to my horror, I saw it skidding violently towards us. Instinctively I pressed my left foot forward to protect my right hip. The truck hit us with a sickening thud. I looked down; my left leg had broken between the knee and ankle and was bent ninety degrees. There was also a sharp pain in my bad hip. I thought that I was having a nightmare and would awake to find myself back in bed. It was in fact a nightmare, but a waking one.

How I was extricated from the car, carried into the military hospital a few hundred yards away, X-rayed, put immediately under anaesthesia and awoke in agony in a hospital room with my leg and hip both in plaster is something which, even at this distance of time, I find it impossible to describe. The next two days were unadulterated agony. Sheikh Abdullah came to my room in great concern, and ran his hand across my face and head in a gesture of genuine commiseration. My father, when he heard of the accident, insisted that I must be flown down to Bombay immediately. I wanted to wait for a few days until the pain subsided, but he was adamant. An Air Force DC-3 was chartered, and once again I was lifted into it and flown out. The plane stopped to refuel in Delhi where my mother, who had rushed down from Kasauli, met me in a state of shock, unable to speak. I then flew on to Bombay where my father met me at the airport. The eminent orthopaedic experts Dr Kini and Dr Mulgaonkar were called in as soon as I reached 19 Nepean

Road. By then my leg had swollen dangerously, and on re-
moving the plaster under yet more anaesthesia they discovered
it to be a mass of blisters. Had I delayed coming down my leg
might well have had to be amputated.

So once again I was back, not merely to square one but to
minus one. In America only my hip was involved. Now both
bones of my left leg were broken, and my hip had again cracked
under the impact of the accident. Both lower limbs were in
plaster and I was in agony, convinced that destiny was determined not to let me live a complete life. Mercifully, it is not easy
to recall pain, because in this second disaster I perhaps underwent more than comes to an average person during an entire
lifetime. For weeks I was in plaster, but the bones would not
heal. My mother came down from Kasauli, and the big
question was what should be done about the wedding. Asha's
uncle, General Bijaya Shumsher, who was later Nepalese Ambassador in New Delhi, came to Bombay to see how I was.
Obviously the January date would have to be postponed, but
for how long depended upon my condition. Dr Kini and
Dr Mulgaonkar tried several manipulations under anaesthesia
but none of them worked, while the blisters on my broken leg
took several painful weeks to heal under prolonged antibiosis.
After the exhilaration of the short summer of freedom in
Kashmir, I was firmly back in the dumps.

Meanwhile, of course, events in the country were moving
onwards. On 26 January India's new Constitution was adopted.
It was a day of great rejoicing; India had finally emerged as a
full-fledged sovereign republic, and Dr Rajendra Prasad took
over as the first President of India from the outgoing Governor-
General, C. Rajagopalachari. In Bombay there was an unprecedented procession which lasted many hours. Even lying on
my sick bed I felt a surge of happiness in becoming for the first
time a citizen of a sovereign, democratic India. Happily I
belonged to a generation that had not actually wielded power
in the old princely order, so that while I did have a special
attachment to my State this was far outweighed by the pride of
being an Indian. My only regret was that on both crucial occasions, Independence Day in 1947 and now Republic Day in
1950, I should have been prostrate on my back, unable to
participate actively in those historic events.

When my bones stubbornly refused to join, the doctors finally decided that they had to operate. The operation was performed and I came round with a metal strip and six screws in my left leg to balance the metal pin in my right hip. My mother had locked herself into her puja room on the day of the operation with instructions only to be informed after it was all over and I had regained consciousness. It transpired that it was just as well that the metal strip had been used, as the broken bones were proving unusually recalcitrant and I could have spent another year in plaster without them joining. Nature's ways are marvellous, but some help from intelligent surgeons can be invaluable in certain situations.

While I was recovering from the operation, I was also in touch with the State leaders, Sheikh Abdullah and his Deputy Prime Minister, Bakshi Ghulam Mohammad, a very different sort of person who was to play a crucial role in the political developments that lay ahead. Sheikh Abdullah wrote to me from time to time, including from New York where he had gone a second time as member of the Indian Delegation to the United Nations when the Kashmir dispute was still a live issue. Meanwhile, a new date for my wedding had been fixed in consultation with the doctors, who thought I should be in a position to walk again six weeks after the operation. My father was determined that the auspicious date should not upset his racing schedule, and the Pandit, suitably warned, came up with a convenient *mahurat*, 5 March. Asha's grandfather was still Prime Minister of Nepal, the last of the Rana rulers whose dynasty had virtually ruled Nepal for a century. It is a curious coincidence that our two dynasties were founded at almost exactly the same time by Maharaja Gulab Singh and Maharaja Jung Bahadur respectively, and that they came to a close almost simultaneously a century later.

Once the date was set, Asha's parents—General and Rani Sarada Shumsher—along with their five children came down to Bombay and settled in at Kutch Castle, a palatial structure then standing on Nepean Sea Road. Normally we would have gone to Nepal with a bridal procession, but as I was in no condition to travel it was decided to have the wedding in Bombay. While my parents went across to meet Asha and her family, it was considered improper that we should meet again before the actual marriage. A formal betrothal ceremony was held in the staircase hall of Kashmir House, when a representative of the Ranas along with two Nepali Pandits came over with the auspicious saffron *tilak* and the engagement ring.

Gradually I began to get out of bed and started moving around with the help of the walking sticks I had brought from America. As the wedding date approached, the house began filling up with guests and relatives. If the wedding had been in Jammu the whole city would of course have been mobilized, but in Bombay my father restricted the invitees to close relatives only. With his characteristic thoroughness he worked out all the details of the various functions preceding and following the wedding, while my mother concentrated mainly on the shopping.

Not surprisingly, it was with a mixture of pleasure and apprehension that I awaited the big event. Having been brought up an only child and gone to a boys' school, my contact with girls had till then been marginal, and for three years before the wedding my broken bones had kept me effectively demobilized as far as the social circuit went. By the end of February I could just about walk without support, but I was most uncertain of getting through the prolonged wedding ceremonies without collapsing midway. As it turned out, a feudal accessory came to my rescue. The sword, which it is obligatory for the bridegroom to carry at a Rajput wedding, doubled as an effective walking stick without causing undue embarrassment.

A day before the wedding the *Swayamvara* ceremony was held, a celebrated and ancient Hindu tradition where the bride 'chooses' her husband from among an array of suitors. Through the ages the position of women in Hindu society fell steadily with disastrous consequences, but the symbolic ceremony was retained by several communities, especially the Ranas of Nepal. Happily for me, the choice was also whittled down to one, rather like the 'free vote' in many countries when there is only a single candidate in the field. For the *Swayamvara* I wore a long brocade coat, a turban with an emerald head ornament, and a jewelled sword. My father and I drove to Kutch Castle in a huge open car—a Packard belonging to the Thakore Sahib of Dhrol, one of the fattest men in the world. It was the only car I could get into with comfort, and so came in most handy. We were received by General Sarada and General Singha, and escorted into a large hall where Asha—so heavily draped in red brocade that for a moment I thought she was a large bundle of clothes—sat on a chair across the floor from me. Then, to the chanting of Sanskrit verses, Asha got up and garlanded me—the symbolic act of choosing—after which I did the same. Asha was then carried off in a decorated palanquin by Nepali servants and maids, her face remaining fully hidden during the whole ceremony.

The next morning, 5 March 1950, I awoke to the strains of Bismillah Khan and party playing the auspicious *shehnai* in the garden. At the best of times getting married was a bit of a gamble, and here I was going to marry a girl of thirteen whom I had only met once for half an hour in the presence of two sets of parents. It was with some trepidation, therefore, that I donned my wedding clothes—a light pink silk shirt, tight pyjamas, another long brocade coat, a red turban and a set of diamond jewellery. My father was also dressed up for the occasion, wearing his fabulous emerald and diamond crown with a matching sword, along with his medals of which he was always very proud; and all the other members of our party including several former ruling princes also wore brocade. The procession was led by an army band, followed by 24 uniformed servants each carrying a silver tray containing jewellery, clothes, dry fruit and sweets as our presents to the bride, then my father with the other princes, relatives and members of the staff on foot. Finally came my open car, tastefully decorated, in which I sat behind in solitary grandeur. The drive from 19 Nepean Road to Kutch Castle on Nepean Sea Road took just over half an hour. At the entrance to Kutch Castle we were greeted by another band and finally came to a halt in front of the main building, where my father and Asha's father formally embraced —the *milni* ceremony—and other members of the two parties greeted each other.

The various elements of the wedding ceremonies reflected the chivalric tradition of the Rajputs. In medieval days travel was difficult and hazardous, and the danger from hostile clans and bandits was ever present, hence the swords for self-protection. In those days the formal meeting between the heads of the two clans being united in wedlock—exogamy being a strict requirement—was a significant event. All Rajputs trace their ancestry to one of the major clans of Rajputana. Thus our family belongs to the Kachwaha clan whose head was the ruler of Jaipur, while the Ranas traced their ancestry to the Sisodhias of Udaipur. The whole concept of the heavily armed bridal procession coming to the bride's home and returning to their fortress with her safely in tow reflects the compulsions of a bygone age, and yet provides a colourful spectacle that continues down to the present day.

After the *milni* my father and the rest of the party were seated under a spacious and colourful canopy specially erected for the occasion, while I was taken off to the *puja mandap*, the enclosure where the religious ceremonies were to take place. After some preliminary prayers to various deities representing different aspects of the all-pervasive divinity, Asha was carried into the enclosure on a palanquin by eight servants preceded by eight Nepalese maidservants dressed in red sarees and carrying the auspicious whisks made of white horse tails. With her arrival the marriage ceremonies got started, lasting over an hour, with Asha, her parents and myself being the main participants. The actual giving away of the bride is done by the father and mother jointly, unlike in the Western tradition where it is done only by the father.

After this comes the heart of the ceremony when the bride and groom walk seven times round the sacred fire, which symbolizes the divine witness to the sacrament of marriage. Asha walked so fast that all I could do was keep up with her, using my trusty sword as a walking stick, and my father had to get up and whisper to her to walk more slowly. After the circumambulation we went through a charming little Nepalese ceremony where the newly-married couple have to sit on a bed and play a game of dice with long, ivory pieces. Even before he announced the result I could see from the triumphant look on the face of the Nepali head priest that Asha had won hands down.

After the wedding ceremony was over all of us drove back to Kashmir House, leaving Asha at Kutch Castle. The next day was the auspicious time for the bride to enter her new home. I came back to the Castle and, after more ceremonies, we finally drove off together to 19 Nepean Road where we were greeted by my parents and a vast assembly of guests. Before we alighted a huge black goat was lifted over our heads to avert the evil eye, and then we walked up steps into the hall and into a glittering array of tiaras and jewellery worn by my mother and other ladies attired for the occasion. The Governor of Bombay happened to be no other than Raja Maharaj Singh, who many years earlier was for a brief while my father's Prime Minister. He and Lady Maharaj Singh were also there, as well as the Chief Minister of Bombay, B. G. Kher. The Home Minister of the State, Morarji Desai was not present, which was perhaps just as well considering the fact that champagne flowed like water and that, by the time the party broke up in the early hours of the morning, ninety per cent of the guests were in high spirits.

When we finally got up to our room it was almost two in the morning. After we had taken off all our jewels and brocades we realized that we were, in fact, very young strangers. And thus it was that we became man and wife.

Chapter 10

The next few weeks were a hectic round of parties given by us, the Nepalese and mutual friends. At some of these my father would get me to sing. I had kept up an interest in music, and despite the break of several years was able quite easily to recall the ragas and songs I had learnt as a boy. My nineteenth birthday was four days after the wedding, for which Asha gave me a Japanese transistor radio which was quite a novelty at the time. She had turned thirteen only a couple of months before we were married. Looking back, it seems incredible how young we were and how, despite difficulties in adjusting to the new situation, we were able to grow into a happy marriage. For Asha, of course, the change was greater. From one of five children living in a huge joint family she suddenly found herself married to a virtual stranger, in a family with a single son and speaking a language which she hardly knew. On top of this, the attitude of my mother, who was always very possessive towards me, was not nearly as understanding towards her as it should have been. For me, too, the change was a major one. Having been an only child, brought up virtually alone, the entry of a new person into my life marked a fresh dimension for which I was emotionally and psychologically not fully prepared. To be successful any marriage needs a great deal of mutual adjustment, but in our case this was even more necessary than usual.

For several months my convalescence and marriage had taken my mind away from the political problems in the State, but the time now came when I had to get back to the job of being Regent. It was decided that we would leave Bombay on 28 April. Bombay was warming up, and my mother, who never liked the heat, decided that she would go back to Kasauli. My father was upset at this, as he had perhaps assumed that after the wedding she would stay on. She decided to leave three days before we were to go. I still remember her coming down the stairs of Kashmir House the evening her train was leaving, and bowing low to my father with folded hands as she said goodbye. What I did not know at the time was that they were never destined to meet again.

Asha and I, along with our staff and servants, left Bombay in a chartered DC-3 early in the morning. We were in Delhi at ten, where we broke journey to call on Sardar Patel who was then at 1 Aurangzeb Road. He was very ill, but he made a special effort to spend some time with us and seemed genuinely pleased to see us. Considering that in a way he was instrumental in arranging our marriage, we thought the least we could do was to stop over and pay him our respects. Jawaharlal was not in Delhi at that time, so we could not see him. We had lunch at the Nepalese Embassy with the Ambassador, Asha's grand-uncle, and then flew on to Jammu which we reached exactly at four. There a truly massive reception awaited us. Apart from Bakshi Ghulam Mohammad and other officials, the whole of Jammu city seemed to have turned out for the welcome and the huge crowds were extremely enthusiastic and affectionate.

The day after we arrived Sheikh Abdullah came down from Srinagar and hosted a formal reception in our honour in the Mandi Mubarak, the old city palace, at which he made the graceful gesture of presenting me with a diamond *sarpech* for my turban on behalf of the State. There was also a ladies reception and endless callers at the palace. Asha took to the whole *tamasha* like a fish to water, and although she did not know a word of Dogri she seemed to manage rather well with whatever Hindi she had learnt. After a fortnight in Jammu we flew up to Srinagar and I was back at Karan Mahal, this time with a lovely child-wife in tow. Asha was thrilled with the Srinagar house and the glorious weather after the heat and bustle of Bombay and Jammu.

Gradually we began settling down to our new life together. It took me some time to realize that I was no longer simply an individual and that there was someone else who would con-stantly be part of my life and activities. Looking back I find it extraordinary how quickly Asha adapted to the new situation. She began to pick up Hindi, and to coach her in English I engaged Mrs Hanley, an Indian lady brought up by mission-aries in Kashmir and at that time married to the author, Gerald Hanley. Asha showed some interest in painting, so we got Mrs Lilian Purbi, an Englishwoman married to a retired

Kashmiri official, to come over and give her lessons. For my part, I resumed contact with Professor Chaku. One day, while we were discussing some points in political science, he suggested that it might be a good idea if instead of diffuse and desultory studies I were to take up the B.A. course of Jammu and Kashmir University and appear as a private candidate the next year. The idea immediately enthused me, and I started studying with political science, economics and English as my subjects. I owe a debt of gratitude to Professor Chaku for this suggestion, because it enabled me to resume my academic interests and laid the foundations for future specialization. It was probably unique that I was studying to graduate from a University of which I was myself Chancellor.

In addition to the B.A. course, Pandit Parmanand began to come again to teach me Sanskrit. Thus, along with official duties which included making speeches at opening ceremonies and entertaining an unending stream of callers, we launched on a fairly stiff academic programme. I resumed reading my favourite thinkers—Bertrand Russell and Aldous Huxley— and was deeply impressed at the masterly way they took up meaningful ideas and dissected them with clarity and imagination. It struck me then how superior the realm of ideas was to the realm of men; none of the grasping corruption, the crass opportunism, only dazzling concepts moving through the clear mind like a flight of swans on the trackless path of the unknown. I also discovered Plato at this time, and was enraptured. The *Symposium* remains among my favourite books, and though I later turned towards Vedanta I continue to value my early encounter with the great seer of the Western world. In his *Republic* I came across the concept of the philosopher king, and once again my youthful imagination was aroused at the possibility of emulating that great ideal.

Meanwhile political developments continued. On 13 July 1931, during the period when Sheikh Abdullah's Muslim Conference had first launched its anti-Dogra movement, an unfortunate incident of an attack on Hindu shopkeepers had taken place resulting in communal riots and firing by the Dogra police in which several Kashmiris were killed. Since then the National Conference observed this as Martyrs' Day. In 1950 Sheikh Abdullah wanted to make some dramatic announcements on that day in order to gain maximum political mileage, and a month before he sent me for signature two proposals regarding abolition of Jagirdari (the feudal land-grant system) and of landlordism, without any compensation at all. I was in broad sympathy with the measures proposed, but obviously they would adversely affect large sections of people, particularly the non-Muslim population of the State. Vishnu Sahay had come up to Srinagar on a visit, and I thought it would be appropriate to refer the matter to him so that the Government of India could apply its mind to the implication of the proposals. When Sheikh Abdullah reminded me about the papers I informed him about what I had done.

This elicited an angry memorandum in which he roundly took me to task for having referred the matter to the Secretary for Kashmir Affairs. He wrote:

It appears that the obvious limitations of the Constitutional head of the State have escaped the attention of Shri Yuvaraj. The action taken by Shri Yuvaraj is entirely opposed to the spirit of the Proclamation dated 5th March 1948 under which the present Government was set up. It has all along been understood that the Ruler or his Regent will act strictly as the Constitutional head of the State and it is on this distinct understanding that the present government hold their office.

He went on, significantly, to add:

It is also clear that the subjects in regard to which the submissions were made did not relate to a matter in which the State had acceded to the Dominion of India and, therefore, in the existing constitutional set up the Government of India has no jurisdiction in this matter.

This was a fairly stiff broadside, but I decided not to buckle under. Vishnu Sahay had earlier flown down to Delhi with the two proposals, so I sent an ADC down post-haste with Sheikh Abdullah's angry note and asked Sahay to consult the 'high command', which in effect meant Jawaharlal, Sardar Patel and Gopalaswami Ayyangar, and let me have a draft reply. He came back the next day with a draft which I appended to the Sheikh's memo and sent back to him on 12 July. It read as follows:

I appreciate the Constitutional position under the Proclamation of March 5, 1948. None the less it seems to me that these very far reach-

ing proposals, which will drastically affect the economy of very large
sections of the population and for the sanctioning of which there is no
properly functioning legislature at present, should, in the existing
delicate political situation, be first examined in concert with the
Government of India, and that we should not rush this legislation
without satisfying that Government.

I would ask the Ministry to consider this aspect of the matter.

Despite this, on the next day Sheikh Abdullah made a long
speech at Lal Chowk in Srinagar in which he went ahead and
announced the measures, despite the fact that he had been
called to Delhi to discuss the matter and that the measures were
not legal without my signature. This was the first of a series of
differences of approach and opinion between him and the
Government of India that grew over the next few years and
culminated in the dramatic events of August 1953. From the
very beginning I looked upon my role as Head of State from one
single angle—how best I could help to safeguard the national
interest in the State as reflected in the positions taken from time
to time by the Government of India under Jawaharlal Nehru.
Evidently my refusal to sign these proclamations came as a rude
shock to the Sheikh, as he had expected me to be merely a
rubber stamp. Thus began a divergence of approach and slow
evaporation of goodwill between us. Although the conflict has
often been portrayed as a hangover of the old Kashmiri–Dogra
animosity, the fact is that, although proud of my Dogra
heritage, I tried to function not so much as a Dogra but as an
Indian. Indeed, it would be correct to say that the basic difference between Sheikh Abdullah and me lay in the fact that
while he looked upon himself as a Kashmiri who happened to
find himself in India, I considered myself an Indian who
happened to find himself in Kashmir.

There was also the still undetermined question of the exact
status of Jammu and Kashmir. I have recorded how my father
was vaguely attracted to the idea of an independent State, but
was overwhelmed by rapidly changing circumstances. Despite
all that had happened subsequently, including the accession,
the war, the ceasefire and the United Nations intervention, the
Sheikh too was by no means averse to the concept of independence. This became amply clear over the next two or three
years, and the now public State Department papers which

speak of the U.S. Ambassador Loy Henderson's discussions with
him in the summer of 1950 only confirm what is well known.
Before he could move in that direction, however, Sheikh Abdullah realized that he had to eliminate all vestiges of Dogra rule
and gather absolute power in his own hands. It was to this end
that he turned his attention with single-minded ruthlessness,
aided and abetted by a host of aides and advisers led by Mirza
Afzal Beg, the Revenue Minister who played Todar Mal to his
Akbar.

In this murky situation my only strategy was to keep in close
touch with the Government of India and to maintain personal
contacts with Jawaharlal. Soon after the proclamations episode,
Asha and I went down to Delhi. Asha drove up to Kasauli to
visit my mother, while I stayed for a few days at Teen Murti
House as a guest of Jawaharlal. Padmaja Naidu was also living
there at the time, and she was always great fun, immediately
putting me at ease by striking up an amusing conversation.
Indira Gandhi was hostess, courteous but rather withdrawn
and uncommunicative. Rajiv and Sanjay were very small at the
time, and I recall walking with Jawaharlal in the back lawn of
the house while he showed his grandchildren the giant pandas
that had recently come as a gift from China.

Sardar Patel had only a few months left and it was not
possible to meet him frequently. I did, however, start regular
meetings with the President, Dr Rajendra Prasad. A kindly and
cultured man, he always received me with affection and listened
with interest to my reports on the situation in the State. It was
clear that his approach was closer to the Sardar's than to
Jawaharlal's, and he was particularly concerned about the difficult position in which the Hindus of the State were placed. He
seemed to share the Sardar's deep reservations about Sheikh
Abdullah, but was far too gentle to express them unequivocally.
It was Dr Rajendra Prasad who came up to Srinagar later that
season to address the second convocation of the University at
which I once again presided.

Although the proclamation problem regarding Jagirdari and
land reforms had been sorted out after Sheikh Abdullah grudg-
ingly made some amendments on the advice of New Delhi, in
which Sardar Patel even in his last weeks took an interest, it
soon became clear that this had been only the opening gambit

in his carefully planned strategy to consolidate his position and gain overriding constitutional legitimacy. It must be remembered that at the time the Kashmir issue was still a live one at the United Nations, where Jawaharlal's overriding idealism and sense of fair play had made the whole matter embarrassingly complicated for India. Using the leverage of the proposed plebiscite, Sheikh Abdullah continued his relentless drive against my father. Not content with having had him exiled from the State, he now began to press for the formal abolition of the ruling dynasty. And the mechanism he chose for this was the concept of a Constituent Assembly for the State. The snag, however, was that such an Assembly could not legally come into existence without my approval.

The concept of the Constituent Assembly to frame a constitution for the State was part of a broader political strategy to make the question of plebiscite redundant. Although on several occasions Jawaharlal reassured the U.N. and Pakistan that India stood by her earlier commitment, it was clear that if a Constituent Assembly did meet and reaffirm the State's accession to India it would have an impact on public opinion abroad. For Sheikh Abdullah, of course, it also provided an excellent opportunity to strike a final blow at the Dogra dynasty and thus fulfil his life's most cherished ambition. During the whole of 1950 there were discussions about this between the State Government and the Union Ministry for Kashmir Affairs. Although my father had designated me as Regent, he had not abdicated and still remained legally the ruler. It therefore became incumbent upon the Government of India to consult him about the Constituent Assembly, and on 30 November 1950 Vishnu Sahay, Secretary for Kashmir Affairs, wrote to him enclosing a draft proclamation to be issued by me and asking for his comments. On 10 December my father wrote a long letter to Sardar Patel in which he made several points which he summarized as under:

1. That the Proclamation, with the object and spirit of which I wholeheartedly agree, should be issued by me as Ruler who is the properly constituted authority in law to promulgate it and not by my Regent.
2. The powers and functions of the body intended to be constituted should be express, well defined and accurately worded and should

exclude from the purview of their inquiry and consideration matters not expressly entrusted to them.

3. They should report to the authority that constitutes them, that is the Ruler who shall seek the advice of the Parliament of India in the matter.

Seen in the light of the remarks made above it will be evident that the Proclamation as drafted if issued would lack proper sanction and will be ultra vires as its various clauses conflict with each other and with the accepted constitutional principles and in actual working of the scheme envisaged will present serious difficulties defeating the very object which it is intended to achieve.

He also wrote to me saying that as he was taking the matter up with the Government of India I should not sign the proclamation until the matter had been clarified.

Soon thereafter Sardar Patel passed away, leaving a vacuum in national life that could never really be filled. On 25 January Vishnu Sahay wrote to me enclosing a copy of the proclamation and suggesting that when I received a 'submission' from Sheikh Abdullah in this regard I should sign it. This submission came on 27 January and read as follows:

The present State Government has always been committed to the position that it is for the people of the State to draw up a constitution of the State, in whatever way they like, and that for this purpose a Constituent Assembly was to be convened at the appropriate time. The Ruler also supported this idea and in the Proclamation issued on 5th March, 1948 provision was made for convening a National Assembly when the normal conditions were restored. In October, 1949 the Government, after taking note of the present conditions and in consultation with the Government of India, decided that the time had come for the setting up of this Constituent Assembly and in pursuance of this decision steps were taken for preparation of the electoral rolls in the State. It was, however, considered desirable that a Proclamation should be issued for convening a Constituent Assembly in the State and that clauses (4) to (6) of the Proclamation, dated 5th March, 1948, superseded, as they did not meet the present requirements. The terms of this Proclamation and the powers and functions of the Constituent Assembly have been the subject of discussion and correspondence with the Government of India for a long time and the Prime Minister feels gratified that in the end a complete agreement has been reached between the views of this Government and those of the Government of India in this respect. The enclosed draft Proclamation has been prepared jointly by the two Governments and has the full concurrence of the Government of India. The Government of India desire that this Proclamation should be issued at as early a date as possible. It is, therefore, requested that the draft Proclamation may be returned forthwith after Shree Yuvaraj has affixed his signature to it.

S. M. Abdullah
PRIME MINISTER
27.1.1951

These developments put me in an acute dilemma. On the one hand was the express direction from my father that I should *not* sign the proclamation, and on the other both the Government of India and Sheikh Abdullah were urging me to sign it. I decided to fly at once to Delhi where I met Gopalaswami Ayyangar, who had taken over as Minister for States, and explained the position to him. On my return I made the following note upon Sheikh Abdullah's submission:

PRIME MINISTER

As you are aware, I derive my powers from His Highness' proclamation dated 20th June 1949, appointing me Regent.

The draft proclamation which you have now put before me is a very important document, involving, as it does, far reaching consequences to the future of the State. The Ministry of States had sent a draft proclamation to His Highness for his comments. His Highness sent his comments thereon to the then Hon'ble Minister for States (the late Sardar Patel), and at the same time directed me not to append my signature on any proclamation on the subject without his express approval.

You will, therefore, appreciate that as I have received no such approval from him yet, I am at this stage precluded from signing the document you have submitted to me. I therefore suggest that you ask the Government of India to pursue this matter with His Highness.

Karan Singh
REGENT
30.1.1951

This put the ball back in the Government of India's court. Meanwhile my father took legal opinion from a leading firm of lawyers, Kanga and Company, which formed the basis of a detailed memorandum that he later submitted to the President. The opinion upheld the view that he remained Ruler who alone had the power to sign a proclamation for the setting up of the Constituent Assembly. Unfortunately the question involved was not one of legal niceties but the harsh realities of political power. V. P. Menon met my father in Bombay, and then on 5 April Gopalaswami Ayyangar wrote a letter to him in which the position was bluntly stated as under:

. . . Developments have, however, since taken place both in the State and at Lake Success which make it imperative that the issue of this Proclamation is not delayed any longer. The Government of India are committed to the convening of a Constituent Assembly, the preparations for which are in active progress in the State. That Assembly will be held whether the formal Proclamation issues or not. In the view of the Government of India it must be convened, if both their commitments to the people of Kashmir and their stand at Lake Success are to be implemented, in spirit and in the letter. From the beginning, they have held that this Constituent Assembly should be called under the provisions of the Constitution of India and that this should be done, from both a tactical and constitutional point of view, on the authority of a Proclamation issued by the Head of the State. The draft of the Proclamation has been agreed between the Government of India and the Government of Jammu & Kashmir. No purpose will, therefore, be served by any act of Your Highness which holds up the signing and issue of this Proclamation by Shri Yuvaraj.

On neither of the two matters about which I can understand your entertaining apprehensions, namely, the continuance of the accession of the Jammu & Kashmir State or of part thereof to India and the connection of the Headship of the State with your dynasty, no *final* decision should be taken by the Constituent Assembly to be convened. They are essentially matters which could be decided only as a matter of agreement between the Government of India and Parliament on the one side and the Government of Jammu & Kashmir and the State Constituent Assembly or legislature on the other. The Government of India will, no doubt, at the proper time take the decision on these matters, which, I need hardly assure you, would be essentially just from the standpoint both of your dynasty and the people of the State. You have obviously to put your trust in the people of the State and the Government of India in respect of this matter. I hope, therefore, you will immediately lift the ban which you have placed on Shri Yuvaraj affixing his signature to the agreed Proclamation and which naturally has placed him in great embarrassment. . . .

This persuaded my father to fall in line, and he wrote to me formally saying that he lifted the ban and left the matter to my discretion. A few days thereafter I received a letter from V. P. Menon urging me to sign the proclamation, which I did on 21 April. Meanwhile, Sheikh Abdullah had evidently not taken kindly to my earlier refusal to sign. In order to keep up the pressure he launched a bitter personal attack on my father and me at a public meeting a few miles from Jammu on 9 April. He again accused my parents of instigating communal riots in 1947 and said that if I was not careful I would also have to go the way he went. This utterly unprovoked attack came as a shock to me, and I immediately wrote to him and sent a copy to Jawaharlal who had just returned from Kashmir, with a covering letter in which I added: 'I am very deeply hurt at Sheikh Sahib's making such remarks in public, particularly as they were not based on facts and were consequently highly misleading.'

The Sheikh responded to my letter with a long five-page epistle in which he made it clear that he expected me to act virtually as a captive of his Government, even to the extent of consulting him before making public appearances. This letter revealed that although he might tolerate me as Head of State, he was incapable of overcoming his pathological aversion to my family. At the time he was riding the crest of the wave, however, and there was little I could do except to lie low for the time being. I kept up my contacts with Jawaharlal. Every time I went to Delhi I would meet him, and he would talk at length on many matters. Kashmir was always uppermost in his mind, and many of his letters to me at that period deal in detail with various internal and international developments relating to the State. It seems that he had developed some affection for me, because he always seemed genuinely pleased to see me. In a letter of 13 May 1951 to my mother he ended by saying: 'I have seen Tiger from time to time and have grown to like him very much. He is a fine young man and I think his good qualities will enable him to face difficulties. I shall certainly help and guide him in every way.'

I quote this because it has a bearing on developments that subsequently took place, and also because it shows that, despite Sheikh Abdullah's special position, it was not as if the other point of view was not being listened to by Jawaharlal. D. P. Dhar also had direct access to Jawaharlal, and between us we were able to counteract to some extent the belligerent Muslim Kashmiri chauvinism represented by the Sheikh and the hard-liners in the National Conference led by Mirza Afzal Beg. Jawaharlal's psychology in this regard was interesting. If he rejected a person's bona fides, then any view or advice from those quarters would at once be suspect. Thus he had a parti-cular dislike for the Praja Parishad leaders in Jammu, because he thought they were communalists and that their actions only jeopardized India's position *vis-à-vis* Kashmir. But if he trusted someone—and he was loyal to a fault as far as his friends were concerned—he would give a careful hearing to their views even if they were not in tune with his own thinking.

Jawaharlal visited Srinagar early in June that year. Evidently Sheikh Abdullah had spoken to him about our brush a few weeks earlier as a result of his Jammu speech, and had suggested that a Secretary should be appointed on my staff. Jawaharlal wrote to me about this from Chashmashahi House where he always liked to stay. The house belonged to us and it was here that my mother and father had been married in 1928. Sub-sequently it was used as a sort of special guest house, and Sir Tej Bahadur Sapru would stay there for several summer weeks along with members of his family. Later it was the residence of Swami Sant Dev, and after 1947 it became the favourite residence of Jawaharlal. The house commands a magnificent view of the Dal Lake, the Shankaracharya and Hari Parbat hills and the higher mountain panorama behind them. The sunsets are particularly spectacular when viewed from here, and Jawaharlal would often sit quietly on the veranda watching the sun sink below the horizon.

I was meanwhile continuing my preparations for the B.A. examination, while Asha had also begun studying English and Hindi, as well as learning how to paint. Our life was beginning to fall into a pattern. In the mornings we would study with tutors for about two hours, after which I would have some formal meetings with officials or visitors. Two or three times a week we had some people over to lunch, including visiting dignitaries such as foreign ambassadors, United Nations per-sonnel and the local gentry. Asha was beginning to pick up conversational English but was still a little shy, so I had to carry on conversation for both of us, which was often amusing. We would sit opposite each other at the middle of the dining table, with guests ranged on either side according to their listing in the warrant of precedence. Our table took a maximum of sixteen people, so the parties were intimate. Over the years I found these meals of real value, because a broad spectrum of people— some highly intelligent and stimulating—came from various parts of India and many other countries of the world. Always a quick learner, I picked up valuable general information and ideas from those conversations.

Apart from being interested in ideas, I found myself drawn towards education, and this led me to suggest to my father that we should donate Gulab Bhavan, our main palace in Srinagar, to the newly established Jammu and Kashmir University. I mentioned this to Jawaharlal and Gopalaswami Ayyangar, who reacted favourably. Jawaharlal wrote: 'I am very glad to learn that you intend donating the Gulab Mahal Palace to the University of Jammu and Kashmir. That is the very best use you can put the building to and I am sure it will be greatly appreciated by the public.' My father was out of India at the time, but his Private Secretary, Bhim Sain Mahey (brother of the communist leader Dhanwantari Mahey), had come to Srinagar and I had asked him to convey my views regarding this donation to my father. Evidently he did not do so, but Gopalaswami Ayyangar meanwhile wrote to my father mentioning the offer and urging him to accept it. My father was furious and wrote me an angry letter. I wrote back, laying out the factors which had impelled me to suggest the gift and summed this up by saying:

Considering all these factors—a fast deteriorating building which is ideally suited to be a University and which is lying neglected and unused, and the fact that our University greatly requires a suitable building and that education is as noble and as worthy a cause as can possibly be found—I sincerely feel that it would be a magnificent gesture on your part if you were to donate the building. The effect of such an act on the public would, I am convinced, be electrifying.

My father, however, disagreed and in his reply angrily said that

9

The Jammu and Kashmir Government have gone out of their way to harass me personally and to humiliate the dynasty in the eyes of the public. . . . I hope you will realize that the gift in the present circumstances with however lofty ideals behind it would be misconstrued as one more instance of the Ruler being proved a non-entity and of no consequence.

And there, for the time being, the matter rested. Soon thereafter Gulab Bhavan was converted into a beautiful hotel, providing tourists to Kashmir with top-class accommodation for the first time. However, I did not forget my commitment to the University, and some years later donated a 120-acre orchard near Hazratbal (named Amar Singh Bagh after my grandfather) to Kashmir University, where the present campus stands on a magnificent site.

Towards the end of October I sat for the B.A. examination. As I was Chancellor, the University authorities offered to open a special centre at my residence, but I thought that would be most inappropriate and decided to take the examination along with other students at the Sri Pratap College centre. The only concession was a higher chair and desk than provided for others, as I had difficulty sitting at a low desk on account of my stiff hip.

On 5 November 1951 the Jammu and Kashmir Constituent Assembly met. Elections to this august body that I had summoned by proclamation had been held earlier, but the only effective opposition group—the Praja Parishad in Jammu—virtually boycotted the elections. As a result of this, 72 out of the 75 members were elected unopposed on the National Conference ticket, and three Praja Parishad members were elected, including the veteran and widely respected leader Pandit Prem Nath Dogra. I did not attend the opening session, but for Sheikh Abdullah, of course, it was his finest hour and he played it to the hilt. In a somewhat pompous and flamboyant opening address in which, among others, he quoted Thomas Aquinas, he pointed out that, apart from framing a Constitution 'for the future governance of the country', the Assembly would declare its 'reasoned conclusion regarding accession' and also deal with the land reforms passed by the Government. He added with relish: 'Another issue of vital import to the nation involves the future of the Royal Dynasty'. After a long description from his point of view regarding the historical background of the Dogra dynasty and its performance, he launched a broadside against my father. He said:

After the attainment of complete power by the people, it would have been an appropriate gesture of goodwill to recognize Maharaja Hari Singh as the first Constitutional Head of the State. But I must say with regret that he has completely forfeited the confidence of every section of the people. His incapacity to adjust himself to changed conditions and his antiquated views on vital problems constitute positive disqualifications for him to hold the high office of a democratic Head of the State.

In the next two paragraphs, however, he came out strongly in favour of my being chosen the first Head of the State. This is what he said:

I am sure none of us is interested in a personal controversy with the Maharajah's family. In the conduct of public affairs, it is necessary that an impartial view of every individual's deeds should be taken. Our judgement should not be warped by ill-will or personal rancour. During our association with Yuvaraj Karan Singh these last few years, I and my colleagues in the Government have been impressed by his intelligence, his broad outlook and his keen desire to serve the country. These qualities of the Yuvaraj single him out as a fit choice for the honour of being chosen the first Head of the State.

There is no doubt that Yuvaraj Karan Singh in his capacity as a citizen of the State, will prove a fitting symbol of the transition to a democratic system in which the ruler of yesterday becomes the first servant of the people, functioning under their authority, and on their behalf.

Clearly this had been the compromise worked out during the long discussions conducted with Jawaharlal and other representatives of the Government of India. This was a shrewd move, on the one hand to avoid offending the Dogras irretrievably and on the other of retaining in a subtle way the constitutional authority of our family. After all, the legal and constitutional validity of Jammu and Kashmir's accession to the Indian Union rested upon the Instrument of Accession signed by my father, and now that very person was being unceremoniously pushed out by an Assembly which had been convened through a proclamation signed by me as his son and Regent! A piquant constitutional impasse was therefore caused by what both Sheikh Abdullah and Jawaharlal thought was an overriding political compulsion to totally eliminate my father from the political scene. In this unusual situation I fitted neatly into the picture and provided all concerned with some sort of a face-saving device.

Howsoever neat the solution, though, the fact remained that it would only work if I agreed to it. And this put me, at the age of just under twenty-one, in the toughest of the many dilemmas that I had faced in my short but exciting political career thus far. Subsequently I have on many occasions been forced to take difficult and major decisions, but this one remains in my memory as the most excruciating of them all.

Chapter 11

The controversy regarding whether or not I should accept the office of elected Head of State after the abolition of the monarchy rapidly gained momentum, specially in Jammu. Already outraged at the way my father had been exiled after having signed the Accession, in sharp contrast to the Nizam of Hyderabad who continued to reside in his State although his government had defied the new Indian republic and even resorted to arms against it, the people of Jammu reacted sharply to the anti-Dogra attitude and speeches of Sheikh Abdullah and his colleagues. In fact, after Independence the ruling families all over India were fading out and had lost effective power, but Sheikh Abdullah's move in making a major drama of 'abolishing' our dynasty was extremely galling to the Dogras. That I should accept to be the first 'puppet' Head of State under these circumstances was looked upon by many as a traitorous act which would lend an aura of legitimacy to the Sheikh's actions. My father himself was justifiably furious at the way he had been treated. Having reluctantly agreed to appoint me Regent, the idea that I would take over as Head of State after he had been unceremoniously abolished *in absentia* was highly unpalatable to him, and it was only after the dramatic events of 1953 that he became partially reconciled to the situation.

Looking back over the years, I can well understand his sentiments. However, several factors weighed with me at the time apart, perhaps, from some deep psychological urge to prove that I could make it on my own. One was my conviction that, whether or not I accepted the office, the Sheikh was determined to push ahead; and if I declined he would simply proceed to elect someone else instead. In fact, the name of Mahasha Nahar Singh, a Harijan member from Poonch, had already been floated in some National Conference quarters. Thus my declining would merely mean that I would have to follow my father into exile in Bombay, because the Sheikh would hardly have tolerated my presence in the State as a potential focus of Dogra resistance and discontent. Not only was the prospect of living permanently in Bombay far from attractive, it would also have meant snapping the last link of our family with the State. I had no doubt that if I left, there being no other member of the family, the Sheikh would in due course proceed to take over all our property and lands, as also the religious and family Trusts set up by my forefathers.

Apart from personal factors, however, there were the broader implications in the whole matter that affected the national interest. I realized that by staying on in the new capacity I might be able to play a useful role in safeguarding and serving the national interest in this sensitive and crucial State, and this obviously was what Jawaharlal Nehru wanted. Thus, once again, the conflict between my father and Jawaharlal became the central feature of my life. Tremendous pressure was brought to bear upon me through various members of my father's staff and senior Dogra leaders. It was pointed out that if I accepted the office it would be tantamount to selling the Dogras out to the Kashmiris; that I would go down in history as a traitor to the dynasty founded by Maharaja Gulab Singh; that if I defied my father I might well be disinherited and lose my patrimony worth many crores of rupees.

In addition to these direct assaults there were more insidious arguments. How did I know the whole arrangement was not some elaborate trap prepared by Abdullah? In the light of his pathological hatred for the family would he not, having secured the abolition of the dynasty with my connivance, seize upon some excuse or the other to turn against me soon and send me packing? Had he not only recently publicly fulminated against me in his Jammu speech, and what was there to prevent him making my position so difficult that I would be forced to quit or face total humiliation? Had the Sheikh not forced the Government of India to resile step by step from all the commitments made to my father, and would he not do the same for any fresh ones that may be made in regard to myself?

I was thus faced with an awesome dilemma, to accept or not to accept. In such a situation, my instinct was to try and gain time, and this I proceeded to do on one very strong ground. Sheikh Abdullah's Government was in the process of detailed negotiations with the Government of India regarding the new constitutional arrangements, covering not only the headship of

the State but other vital matters such as citizenship, fundamental rights, the Supreme Court, financial integration, the
flag, the powers of reprieve of the President and other allied
matters. Jawaharlal wrote to me about these matters on 26 July
1952 in which, *inter alia*, he said:

> I am sure you will appreciate what I am writing. I need not tell you
> that now and later, you will be in mind and you can always come to
> me for advice or any help that I can give you. The best advice is to
> accept cheerfully and willingly the changes suggested and thereby to
> put yourself in the forefront of them, instead of appearing as if you
> unwillingly agreed to something that you disliked. If we have to do
> something, we should do it gracefully and thereby gain the goodwill
> and respect of others.

In reply I seized upon what I thought was a persuasive
argument. I said:

> Before I proceed, I would like to express my deep gratitude to you
> for the kind and sympathetic interest you have been taking in my
> affairs during the last three years or so since I became Regent. I need
> hardly express how greatly I value your guidance and advice.
>
> As regards the question of whether I should or should not accept a
> five-year elected term as Head of State, I have—since your speech in
> Parliament was delivered about ten days ago—been giving the matter
> my most thorough consideration from all its various aspects.
>
> My highest ambition is to be able to serve effectively the people of
> my country, and any position which gives me that opportunity will
> naturally be welcomed. However, in the present circumstances, I feel
> that it is not possible for me to come to any decision until the new
> Constitution for Kashmir emerges in its final shape from the Con-
> stituent Assembly and receives the approval of the Government of
> India. I am sure you will appreciate that it is hardly possible for me to
> accept a position without knowing exactly and clearly the duties and
> functions which attach to it, the responsibilities which I will have to
> shoulder and the conditions under which I will have to work.

Soon thereafter Sheikh Abdullah called on me and reiterated
that I must take an early decision as to whether or not I would
accept to be Sadar-i-Riyasat. I tried to press my arguments but
he brushed them aside, saying that the Constitution might take
considerable time in drafting and he was not prepared to wait
till then. I wrote again to Jawaharlal protesting against this
attitude. Some days later he replied on 8 August in a three-page

letter. Regarding my point of waiting until the whole Constitution was drafted he said:

I quite agree with you that this business of hustling through a part of the Constitution is neither normal nor ordinarily desirable. The proper course would have been to pass the full Constitution and then give effect to it. But this matter was discussed by us at very great length when the Kashmir delegation was here and ultimately we came to the conclusions which were embodied in the points of agreement. It serves little purpose to go back on them and renew the old argument. Much has been done which cannot be undone at the present stage and any attempt to do so would only produce further complications. Therefore, we have to accept the present position as it is. That is to say that a part of the Constitution dealing with the Head of the State, in the form agreed upon, should be adopted first.

And he ended with the following advice:

The alternative to your not accepting this will not only be bad for the State but will be of no advantage to you at this stage. You mentioned to me your desire for education abroad. A year or more abroad may do you good no doubt. But we learn more about life and its problems by facing them than by mere changes in geographical environment. You are likely to have a fair amount of time at your disposal for study. You are attracted to it and you can thus prepare yourself in many ways better in the State than if you went abroad. Most foreign countries today are full of the noise of war and its preparations and are not very pleasant places to go to except for brief visits.

I feel, therefore, that it would be the right thing for you to accept the offer in the manner I have suggested and thereby put yourself right with your people and do them much service in many ways which may not be so obvious and yet which are important. And then, after all, you retain your freedom of choice at any later moment, should occasion so demand.

I decided to go down to Delhi and discuss the matter personally. Jawaharlal as usual greeted me with great affection in his gracious drawing-room in Teen Murti. He was then at the height of his power, and spoke gently but with great conviction. He explained to me why he and his colleagues were anxious that I should accept. Evidently the Sheikh's constitutional negotiating team consisting of himself, Mirza Afzal Beg, D. P. Dhar and M. A. Shahmiri, his constitutional adviser, had taken rigid positions, because for the first time I noticed a slight hint of displeasure in Jawaharlal's remarks about Sheikh Abdullah. Although he did not say so in so many words, I gathered the distinct impression that he wanted me to be on the scene so that I could be of help if some difficulty arose in the future. When I explained to him my difficulty regarding Jammu opinion he agreed that I might invite some Jammu leaders to Srinagar for consultations. This itself was a major shift in view of his well known allergy to the Praja Parishad, and reflected the fact that he appreciated my difficulty.

It was on this visit that, at a tea party hosted by Jawaharlal in the lawns of Teen Murti, I came across C. Rajagopalachari who was then Chief Minister of Madras. Having met him once when he was Governor-General several years earlier, I went up and greeted him. 'You may not remember me,' I said, 'I am Karan Singh.' He turned round, looked at me and said, 'Of course I remember you. You have got such beautiful eyes.' It is not often that I find myself at a loss for words, but at that moment I was rendered speechless. I also called on Maulana Azad, who was the epitome of culture and erudition and whose conversation was always a joy.

On my return to Srinagar I began the process of consulting the Jammu leaders, including the President of the Praja Parishad, Pandit Premnath Dogra. After the meeting he issued a statement reiterating the demand for complete accession and concluding that 'till the new Constitution for the State assumes a concrete shape, it would be premature to give any definite opinion on this single issue of accepting the office of the Head of the State by Shree Yuvaraj Bahadur'. In fact, they were strongly opposed to my accepting, but after three days' talks I was able to bring them round to at least this intermediate position. Meanwhile, I learnt that my father had sent a long memorandum to the President, and there were press reports to the effect that he had demanded a referendum in the State upon the issue of retention or abolition of the dynasty.

Early in September I wrote to Jawaharlal reporting on my meeting with the Jammu leaders and pointing out the genuine grievances and apprehensions that they had expressed. I urged that senior Indian leaders—specially Maulana Azad, Dr K. N. Katju, the then Home Minister, and Gopalaswami Ayyangar, the Minister for Kashmir Affairs—should meet the Jammu leaders and give them a sympathetic hearing. I concluded the letter with a mention of my father's reported memorandum and, although I knew Jawaharlal would not be pleased, felt impelled to end with the following paragraph:

I wonder what your view about this is. If it is possible to have a referendum—and I do not see why it should not be—I feel it would be a good thing, as it would give the people of the State a fully democratic method of expressing their decision as to whether they would like a member of the dynasty to be their Constitutional Head or would prefer to elect someone periodically. Thus no section or group will feel that its views have been ignored in coming to a decision on this important question. I must add that from indications both in Jammu and in the valley I feel that the result of such a referendum is by no means a foregone conclusion.

Jawaharlal replied the very next day. While accepting that the Jammu people have a number of grievances, some of which were justified, he went on to castigate the Praja Parishad for their mode of functioning. About the memorandum, he wrote: 'I have seen the long memorandum which your father has sent to the President. There is no reference in it to a referendum. The memorandum is rather an angry and tendentious document. Your father does not seem to realize at all that the world has changed and is changing rather rapidly.'

He then concluded with some comments on my mention of a referendum. He wrote:

I am rather surprised at your reference to the referendum. This is not at all possible either from the local or from the international point of view. We have been talking about the plebiscite over other issues and even this cannot come off because there is no agreement. If the question of a referendum on a limited issue was raised, this would immediately lead to all kinds of international complications and the demand for a plebiscite immediately over the wider area. Even this referendum, it would be said, if held at all, should be over that wider area, including that part which is held by Pakistan. Within the present boundaries of the State under our control the referendum issue would, naturally, lead to bitterness and controversy and in effect tend to split up the State, regardless of the final issue. Indeed, I think that such a proposal is completely out of court in the present circumstances. Pakistan would, no doubt, profit by it, but no one else.

At about this time, I had the dramatic experience of accompanying Jawaharlal on a flight to a newly constructed airfield at Chushul in Eastern Ladakh. This was situated at an altitude of 14,270 feet above sea level, reportedly the highest airfield in the world. On the flight were Indira Gandhi, Sheikh Abdullah and several others, and we were piloted by the ace flier, Air Marshal Mehr Singh. We flew in a DC-3 at an altitude of over 20,000 feet and wore oxygen masks most of the way. The sight of the great Himalaya from the air was spectacular, the mountains looked like some vast, frozen ocean stretching endlessly in all directions. The sight of Nanga Parbat, one of the world's highest peaks, standing lone and majestic, robed in icy splendour was unforgettable. Just before landing at Chushul we flew over a huge turquoise-blue lake, and when we landed I had a strange feeling of sensory distortion. The mountains near the runway looked so close that Indira Gandhi wanted to walk up to them. However, we were told to our astonishment that they were at least ten miles away. In that rarefied air objects looked much nearer than they actually are. We stayed at the airfield for about ninety minutes while Jawaharlal chatted with the air force officers. There was no habitation or vegetation within sight, and the landscape had a stark beauty that might have belonged to another planet.

This flight to Chushul strengthened my earlier desire to pay a visit to Ladakh on my own, and soon after I decided to visit that far-flung region of 36,000 square miles which was annexed to the State by General Zorawar Singh and his intrepid Dogra forces way back in the time of Maharaja Gulab Singh. This represented two-thirds of the entire area of the State left in our possession. No member of our family had ever visited Ladakh, which was administered by a *Wazir Wazarat* (equivalent to Deputy Commissioner) during Dogra rule. It was narrowly saved from falling into the hands of the Pakistani raiders in 1947, and remains the largest Lamaistic Buddhist enclave in the world, Tibet having fallen under Chinese rule in what was one of Jawaharlal's less successful foreign policy exercises.

Asha and I landed in Leh to a rousing reception. The entire population of the town and surrounding villages had turned out to greet us, led by the Head Lama Kushak Bakula. Stepping out of the plane was stepping into another, but friendly world—the deep blue sky, the clear, rarefied air, the Ladakhis in their traditional robes and the women with their gorgeous turquoise headpieces. We were in Leh for three days, during which we visited the leading Buddhist monasteries and made offerings and prayers there. Some of the statues of the Buddha and Bodhisattvas were stunningly beautiful, and the Lamaseries were decorated with freshly painted wooden furniture and hung with priceless scrolls or *thangkas* illustrating various Buddhist deities. Hundreds of white metal cups held oil wicks which imparted a soft, mellow glow to the shrines and this, combined with the deep, continuous chanting by the monks, created a strangely hypnotic effect. I remember in particular the huge hollow metal image of the Buddha at the Shay monastery, three stories high and so large that it was used in earlier times as a grain reservoir for the entire town of Leh.

We had taken with us several thousand yards of cloth for distribution so that every inhabitant of Ladakh could get enough for a coat. It was touching to learn that these pieces were treated with reverence and affection by the people even in far-off villages as tokens from the Dogra ruling family. Quite evidently time had removed any traces of bitterness and left in its place a genuine regard for our family among the Ladakhis. We received several colourful presents, including a set of Ladakhi clothes in which I was photographed. Many years later, when I revisited the Lamaseries I was surprised to see this photograph in almost all of them. Asha was fascinated by the turquoise-studded hair ornaments worn by the Ladakhi women. From Leh we flew to Kargil, the second town in Ladakh and the centre of the area inhabited by Shia Muslims. The Ceasefire Line passed very close to Kargil, and the army here was more in evidence. The brigade headquarters where we stayed were situated on the banks of the Indus. It struck me as curious that although the very name of our country and its predominant religion are derived from the Indus, the only place where this great river now flows through Indian territory is Ladakh.

During my stay in Ladakh I had some serious discussions with Kushak Bakula and his colleagues. Even more so than in Jammu, the Ladakhis were feeling uneasy and insecure under the Sheikh's administration. Forming as they did a distinct

cultural entity, they felt that their position in the new dispensation, with only two members in the State Assembly, on
the basis of population, was extremely precarious and made
them totally subordinate to the Kashmiris. They suggested that
a Statutory Advisory Committee should be set up to which it
should be obligatory for the State Legislature to refer all
legislation vitally affecting Ladakh. They also urged that, instead of leaving them at the mercy of the Sheikh's Government,
an administrator should be sent from the Centre.

On my return to Srinagar I wrote to Jawaharlal enclosing a
note on my impressions regarding Ladakh and suggesting
measures to improve the situation. Urging him to take early
action in the matter I pointed out that 'Ladakh is strategically
very important, more so for India as a whole even than for the
State, and it will be a tragedy if for lack of an accommodating
spirit the people of Ladakh remain unhappy and discontented,
and thus an easy prey to all sorts of exploitation, both com-
munalist and communist.' As usual, Jawaharlal replied within
a week. He said that 'the real difficulty about Ladakh is its
terrible economic backwardness', and concluded his letter with
the remark that 'we should like to make a road to Leh from
Kulu Valley, but this is a very expensive undertaking and for
the present it is difficult to take it up. That road will open out
the mineral deposits of Ladakh and will bring a certain measure
of prosperity to that region.'

It has been my experience that an outer crisis often triggers
off an inner response which may appear totally unconnected
with the visible trend of events. While all these political events
were in progress, a process of inner development was also going
on. I began at this stage to develop a strong predilection for
spiritual ideas. Edwin Arnold's *The Light of Asia*, that great
poem on the life and teachings of the Buddha, had a deep
impact upon me. At about this time I went out to Dachigam
and shot a bear while it was eating mulberries on one of the
trees. It fell to the ground shrieking pitifully like a child, and
lay there for long before it died. Those cries haunted me for
weeks, and as a result I decided to give up shooting and fishing.
Despite my association with these sports from childhood, I have
never since indulged in either of them. It was evidently the
same influence that led me privately to record a signed note on

1 January 1952 to the effect that my long-range aim was 'to achieve spiritual enlightenment and peace, and to successfully spread the message throughout the world so that the world which is rushing headlong into the dark and frightful abyss of destruction along the road of hate, envy, cruelty and fanaticism can be saved and put on the broad and clear sunlit path of peace, happiness, love and universal prosperity'. I was just under twenty-one when I wrote this, and though the impulse remains with me, I have over the years begun to realize that saving the world is not quite as simple a task as it might have appeared then.

Meanwhile my examination results had been announced. I passed the B.A. (missing a first division by six marks) and thus became probably the first Chancellor in world history to graduate from his own University. That year the philosopher-statesman, Dr Radhakrishnan, came to deliver the convocation address. I greatly admired his writings, and the impressive manner in which he put across his ideas in crisp, concise and eloquent sentences, punctuated with quotations from the Sanskrit classics. In fact I decided then to model my public-speaking style on his. That year he gave a brilliant extemporaneous address to the convocation, which was held under the magnificent Chinar trees in the garden of the old city palace on the Jhelum, a setting far more impressive than any auditorium. As Chancellor it was my function to present the certificates to the graduates of the year, but obviously I could not present one to myself. So, after the presentations were over, I stepped down and received my own certificate from Dr Radhakrishnan.

Among the numerous books that I read during this period one deserves special mention, as it introduced me to two personalities who were to have a profound influence on my inner life in the years to come. *Among the Great* by Dilip Kumar Roy is a record of his meetings and interviews with five outstanding world thinkers—Bertrand Russell, Romain Rolland, Mahatma Gandhi, Rabindranath Tagore and Sri Aurobindo. The essay on Sri Aurobindo was particularly interesting, and though I had never met him in person I began to get increasingly drawn to his magnificent vision of a spiritualized human consciousness. More important, the essay made mention of an Englishman called Ronald Nixon who had become a *Vaishnava* sanyasi (a

monk) under the name of Sri Krishnaprem. This finally led me
to the feet of the most remarkable man I have ever had the
privilege of meeting. I thus owe a double debt of gratitude to
Dilipda, and to destiny for having placed his book in my hands
at a critical juncture in my life. Sri Aurobindo and Sri Krishnaprem were to become the twin guiding stars for my inner quest,
converging in the golden notes of the eternal flutist.

The whole question of constitutional developments continued to proceed inexorably. My father had been conducting
prolonged correspondence with the States Ministry, but he and
the Government of India were on such different wavelengths
that the exercise was infructuous. My father kept insisting on
his rights and the solemn commitments given to him from time
to time, while the Minister for States, Dr K. N. Katju, kept
reiterating the changed political conditions in the State and the
broader compulsions of international politics. The Secretary in
the Ministry of States, C. S. Venkatachar, called on my father
in Poona in September, after which my father wrote an
anguished letter to Dr Katju. Referring to the memorandum he
had sent to the President of India he recalled the 'misfortunes
brought about by a persistent disregard of my rights and the
assurances given to me to preserve them by the Government of
India, thereby weakening my position and securing very unfair and undue advantage to my persecutors', and added, 'Am
I not entitled, may I ask you, to be told either that I am wrong
or that the Government of India are committed to carry out a
certain policy emanating from Sheikh Abdullah even though it
may mean sacrificing myself, my dynasty and certain cherished
principles of justice and equity? Have I lost the elementary
rights of a person who considers himself aggrieved and seeks
justice?'

As in some ancient Greek tragedy, however, my father found
the situation implacably moving against him. There was tremendous pressure on him to abdicate, but this he resolutely
refused to do. Ultimately, some other broad matters relating
to his privy purse and privileges were discussed and tentative
formulations arrived at. My own efforts to stall a decision in
the matter were also reaching breaking point, and my hope that

some agreed solution between the Government of India and my father would be worked out, thus clearing the way for my course of action, had also proved illusory. The moment of truth was fast approaching, and I realized that I would soon have to take a decision on my own responsibility and be prepared to face whatever consequences may ensue. There were no soft options, and it was becoming clear to me that the choice was really between bowing out of public life altogether and joining the ranks of former princes who patronized the Bombay race club, or of staying in the fray and fighting it out even if it meant ultimate defeat. It was also a choice between the advice and influence of two men, both powerful and strong-willed personalities.

On 30 October 1952 Jawaharlal wrote me a letter saying that the prolonged discussions with Sheikh Abdullah regarding the Head of State had finally concluded with the agreement that the President should act under Article 370 of the Constitution and vary the explanation given there regarding this office, that it was not desirable to keep the matter pending any longer, and that necessary steps would be taken around the middle of November. 'I hope that you will agree to the steps we have suggested', he wrote. 'That is the only course that is open to us now and we should not hesitate to take it. Any other course or an attempt at postponement will only lead to difficulty and trouble.' Significantly, he added, 'I am afraid your father the Maharaja has not been very co-operative. We have tried to explain matters to him and to help him as far as possible. But he appears to be totally unaware of the changes that have taken place and are taking place in the world, and puts forward some pleas which have no application in the present.'

This crossed a letter I wrote to Dr Katju in which I asked for some clarifications regarding the position and functions of the proposed office of 'Sadar-i-Riyasat', the name given to the office of Head of State under the new Constitution. I sent a copy to Jawaharlal. It is an index of his keen interest in Kashmir affairs that he responded to my letter at once, even before Dr Katju had been able to reply. After dealing briefly with the points I had raised he concluded, 'If you have to start a new relationship, it should be under as favourable auspices as possible and with goodwill. That is a stronger guarantee than anything else.'

Two days later Dr Katju also replied, dealing in detail with various points including the privy purse (reduced from Rs 28 to 10 lakhs and distributed between my father, my mother and myself), the emoluments of the Sadar-i-Riyasat, the flag, the tenure of office, and so on.

Before finally taking the plunge I decided to pay another visit to Delhi. There I called on Jawaharlal as usual. He was deeply aware of my difficulty, and spoke to me at length about the national implications of my decision and of how a person has to take a clear stand at critical junctures regardless of pressures and hesitations. He repeated some of the perplexity that he was beginning to feel in dealing with Sheikh Abdullah, and said that this made it all the more important that I should be on the scene to be able to help if some problems arose in the future. It was this final aspect that clinched the issue as far as I was concerned. Although he asked for no assurance, and I gave him none, I left Teen Murti with my mind made up to accept.

I returned to Srinagar around 12 November. On the 15th the Constituent Assembly met and elected me Sadar-i-Riyasat for a five-year term. I had turned twenty-one only a few months earlier, so the usual constitutional age limitation for Head of State was reduced from 35 to 21 years. Jawaharlal wrote me a semi-formal letter which read as follows:

My dear Yuvraj,

I write to congratulate you on the high honour that has been conferred upon you by the people of Jammu and Kashmir State on your election as Sadar-i-Riyasat. I should like to congratulate the people of the State also on their wise choice. This puts a great responsibility upon you, for you have not merely to follow an established convention but rather to help in making conventions for the future. You know how dear the future of the State is to me. It is dear to me because of my own intimate relationship with Kashmir and it is dear to me also because of the numerous ties that bind the State to India. Our future is linked together and we have to face good fortune and ill-fortune alike together.

A new chapter opens now in the Jammu and Kashmir State. And yet, although it is new, it is a continuation of the old but in a different form. The processes of life, whether that of an individual or of a nation, are both a continuation and a continuous change.

I earnestly hope that the changes that have been brought about in the Constitution of the Jammu and Kashmir State will lead to the greater prosperity and happiness of the people of the State and will bring them even closer to India, of which they are such an intimate part.

To you, who have to shoulder this burden and this responsibility at such an early age, I send all my good wishes and my affection.

> Yours sincerely,
> Jawaharlal Nehru

Characteristically, he appended a small note:

My dear Tiger,

I am sending you separately a semi-formal letter of congratulation and good wishes. I did not quite know how to address such a letter. You know that I shall often think of you and that you can always rely on such help and guidance as I can give.

> Yours
> Jawaharlal Nehru

On the night of the 16th Asha and I sat up into the small hours of the morning. I knew that I had irrevocably severed my links with the feudal system and also that, howsoever cordial our relations would be on the surface, my father would not easily forgive me for accepting the new office. I realized that the Sheikh was an inveterate foe of our dynasty and that by accepting it I was virtually placing myself at his tender mercies. I also knew that the reaction among my own community, the Dogras of Jammu, would be hostile, at least to begin with. And yet I was convinced that the old order had passed never to return; that whatever the future might hold there was no future for me or my people unless I threw in my lot with Jawaharlal Nehru and the new India that he had done so much to create and was guiding with such courage and foresight. While I was cutting myself away from the old feudal tradition, I felt that by accepting the new challenge I was also joining the much larger adventure of building and shaping the destiny of a nation representing one-seventh of the human race. The die was cast, and on the morrow I would move onto a fresh stage of my life and destiny.

The next morning, 17 November 1952, I drove to the old Rajgarh Palace on the Jhelum which had been the residence of the former rulers until my father shifted to the Dal Lake. The Darbar Hall with its magnificent papier mâché ceiling, the

symbol *par excellence* of the old order, had been converted into a
legislative chamber for the Constituent Assembly. Where pre-
viously the courtiers had sat on the carpet with only my father
sitting on his gold throne, now benches had been constructed
and the Speaker sat on an elevated platform at the opposite end
of the beautiful hall. It was to this platform that I was conducted, having been received at the entrance by Sheikh
Abdullah, Bakshi Ghulam Mohammad and the Speaker, G. M.
Sadiq. As I entered the hall the assembled members of the
Constituent Assembly stood and applauded vigorously. I was
at once the last representative of the old order becoming, by the
consent of the people, the first servant of the new.

After I took my seat on the dais, flanked by the Sheikh and
his colleagues, the Chief Justice Wazir Janki Nath stood up and
administered the oath of office which I repeated after him.
Then I read out a short speech that I had worked on for several
days in which, *inter alia*, I said:

I am aware that the functions of the Head of a State are, as a focus
of unity, both important and onerous. This is particularly true in a
State where conditions have been as abnormal as they have been here.
I must admit that I had some hesitation in taking upon myself the
responsibilities which this position entails, knowing as I did that there
must be many better fitted than myself both in ability and experience
to fill this office. But the trust and confidence which has now been
placed in me has given me hope and courage to assume these new
responsibilities, and I can assure you that whatever talent and capacity
I might possess will be entirely at the service of the State and its
people.

Our State has, as I have said, been passing through extremely
abnormal times, and over the last few years it has been subjected to
extraordinary strains and stresses. The ruthless and cruel invasion of
our fair country brought in its train untold suffering and misery.
Hundreds were massacred, thousands more were uprooted from their
hearths and homes and thrown into a nightmare of horror and
wretchedness. In the long and chequered history of our land this was
perhaps the greatest crisis that our people were called upon to face and
combat. It is a tribute to them and to their leaders that they rose to the
occasion and met the situation with composure and courage. This
heroic endeavour alone would not have availed, had it not been
firstly for the gallant resistance put up by our forces, isolated and
overwhelmingly outnumbered as they were, and secondly for the

timely aid which was rushed to us by India in that hour of greatest need.

I concluded with the following words:

Our State can be in a position to face all these vital issues only with the united strength of our people. In this land of colour and beauty, men of different faiths and creeds live as the common inheritors of a great past and culture. It is our task now to forge a greater unity among them as the joint architects of their future. Such abiding unity cannot be imposed from above but has to be based upon the interests of the common man in all parts of the State. In building this equal partnership of all the people and all the regions of this State, a solemn duty devolves upon each one of us to do our bit, to make our individual contribution. With your blessings and good wishes I hope to be able to effectively contribute towards this end.

Chapter 12

A week after assuming the office of Sadar-i-Riyasat the Government moved down to Jammu for the winter. The Praja Parishad had of course been outraged at my acceptance of the office, and had threatened a black-flag demonstration on the day I arrived in Jammu. On 24 November I flew down on the Indian Airlines plane. In sharp and poignant contrast to the earlier occasions after my return from America and my marriage, when the people of Jammu gave me an enthusiastic and affectionate welcome, this time there were derisive and hostile slogans, and the city, from the airport right up to the palace gates, was a sea of black flags. Bakshi Ghulam Mohammad was with me in the open jeep, and though the National Conference had tried to lay on some kind of reception it was swamped by the deep hostility of the Dogra masses.

I must admit that it was a rather traumatic experience, but I put up a brave front and continued to smile and greet the people. I noticed that, despite themselves, many waved back. The demonstration, in fact, was not so much against me as a gesture of loyalty to and solidarity with my father. It reflected the widespread agitation launched by the Praja Parishad on 14 November against Sheikh Abdullah. Their slogan of complete integration of the State with India was expressed in the rallying cry '*Ek vidhan, ek nishan, ek pradhan*' (one constitution, one flag and one president). This agitation gathered momentum over the next few months, as it effectively capitalized upon the sense of outrage felt by the Dogras not only at having lost their predominant position in the State but also in having at one stroke been placed at the mercy of their arch enemy, Sheikh Abdullah. The Sheikh, for his part, not only made no effort to mollify the feelings of the Jammu people but continued with his hostile and aggressive attitude. An example was the question of the flag to be flown on the Jammu Secretariat. The old State flag having been hauled down, I had suggested to the Government that, along with the new flag, the national flag should also be hoisted. This was sharply turned down by the Sheikh, and so

I in turn declined the suggestion that I should personally hoist the new flag.

After settling down in Jammu I began assessing the situation, and soon realized that the Praja Parishad agitation had spread deep and wide throughout the Jammu region. Even though I knew Jawaharlal's aversion to the Parishad, I felt it my duty to inform him about the true state of affairs. I prepared a detailed note which analysed the whole position and made certain concrete recommendations for political and economic measures that would help to meet the genuine aspirations of the people of Jammu and Ladakh. As I put it, 'Stripped of all its non-essentials, the situation is that whereas Jammu and Ladakh strongly desire complete integration with India, Sheikh Sahib and his colleagues are extremely insistent upon the "limited" nature of the Accession and are not prepared to agree to complete integration.' This I sent to Jawaharlal with a covering letter on 22 December, following up an earlier one dated 1 December 1952. I was quite frank. 'The situation is serious', I wrote, 'not in any military sense but in the sense that an overwhelming majority of the Jammu province seem to be emphatically in sympathy with the agitation. Fundamentally responsible for this, I feel, are several deep-seated and genuine economic and psychological reasons, and I do not think it will be a correct appraisal to dismiss the whole affair as merely the creation of a reactionary clique.'

I followed this with a visit to Delhi where I talked with Jawaharlal, the Home Minister, Dr Katju and Dr Rajendra Prasad, and gave them my assessment of the situation. I urged that the Government of India must intervene so that the State Government reacts to the Jammu agitation not only with police repression but with concrete political, economic and administrative measures. Jawaharlal did write to Sheikh Abdullah in the same month, who replied with a long letter justifying the stand of his Government and rejecting the whole Jammu problem as the work of communal organizations and a 'violent reaction on the part of Jammu landlords and other upper classes'. Jawaharlal also answered my letter, saying, 'I can quite understand your great concern over the developments in Jammu. I am naturally also very much concerned and I have followed them closely. I entirely agree with you that while police measures are of course necessary, that is only a negative way of dealing with the situation. . . . The situation in Jammu is serious enough to deserve our fullest consideration and such positive action as may be necessary. At the same time, one has to view these matters, as all other important matters, coolly and dispassionately.'

Later that month I received a message from Jawaharlal saying that the President had invited me to attend the Governors and Rajpramukhs Conference being held early in February and that he would like me to attend. This was my first opportunity to attend a meeting on the national level, all my previous experience having been connected only with Jammu and Kashmir. It was, therefore, with some excitement that I accepted the invitation. I arrived in Delhi on 3 February and was put up at Rashtrapati Bhavan in the huge Dwarika Suite reserved for visiting dignitaries. After a formal call on Dr Rajendra Prasad I turned in and went to sleep quite early. I had a curiously vivid dream that night. I was standing in a large room, and Mahatma Gandhi came in. I remember him distinctly, all his features and clothes much clearer in my memory than when I had actually seen him in Srinagar several years earlier. He walked up to me, put his left hand on my shoulder and took my right palm in his other hand. He looked at it for a moment, and then said in English, 'You will be a very wise man'.

I found the two-day Conference itself interesting, the first of a long series of fifteen such consecutive conferences that I was to attend in the future. It opened with a formal speech read out by the President, after which Jawaharlal made an hour-long intervention with a wide ranging survey of the current national and international scene, laying special emphasis upon various aspects of economic development. The scholarly Vice-President, Dr Radhakrishnan, spoke on the second day, brilliantly outlining his views on education and national development. In those days the princely States had yet to be fully integrated into the republic, and were grouped into several geographical zones each headed by a senior prince called the Rajpramukh. The Conference was thus attended by the former rulers of Mysore, Nawanagar, Patiala, Travancore, Gwalior and Jaipur, apart from the Governors who included Chandulal Trivedi, K. M.

Munshi, R. R. Diwakar, Jairamdas Daulatram, Fazl Ali and Pattabhi Sitaramaiyya.

At twenty-two I was, of course, one-third the age of most of the participants. After the general speeches each participant gave a brief report of the situation in his State, highlighting the main problems that they were facing. In my remarks I reviewed the important developments over the last year, and also mentioned the continuing agitation in Jammu. Apart from a formal banquet hosted by the President and attended by Cabinet Ministers, Jawaharlal held a dinner for the participants. He also had me over for a small, private lunch at which Indira Gandhi was hostess and Padmaja Naidu the soul of the party.

Meanwhile the Jammu agitation showed no signs of abating and, in fact, was taken up by like-minded parties in Delhi, specially the newly formed Bharatiya Jan Sangh headed by Dr Shyama Prasad Mukherjee and N. C. Chatterjee, who decided to launch a Satyagraha on an all-India basis. I continued to urge that there should be a dialogue between the State Government and the agitation leaders, but Sheikh Abdullah would have none of it and Jawaharlal was also averse to such talks. As he wrote in one of his letters to me (22 March 1953): 'In my view what these people have done is little short of treason to the country and the people should realize it.' My suggestion to Sheikh Abdullah that my formal address to the Legislative Assembly on 25 March could be used as a good opportunity to strike a conciliating note was rejected by him.

Although Sheikh Abdullah attempted to dismiss the whole matter as the plot of 'reactionary elements', and the Government of India seemed in the beginning to support that view, I was deeply disturbed because I realized that the final chance of building a new Dogra–Kashmiri rapport, which alone could ensure the stability and welfare of the State, was being lost. I continued to dwell on this theme in my letters to Jawaharlal, even though I knew that he was allergic to the Jan Sangh and Praja Parishad leaders. In a letter of 27 March I wrote: 'What really disturbs me is the fact that the gulf between Jammu and Kashmir has widened tremendously over the last few months, and that the breach instead of being bridged seems to be steadily widening. Neither of the parties seems to quite realize the implications of this, and I fear that we may reap a very bitter harvest in years to come.'

At about this time Bakshi Ghulam Mohammad, who was Deputy Prime Minister, and Girdhari Lal Dogra, the Finance Minister and sole representative in the Cabinet from Jammu, met Jawaharlal in Delhi to discuss the whole situation. Bakshi was very different to the Sheikh, more pragmatic, a superb organizer and a man with excellent public relations with all sections of people including many in Jammu. Although closely associated with Sheikh Abdullah and the National Conference, he never displayed the aggressive anti-Dogra attitudes of the Sheikh and M. A. Beg. His whole stance *vis-à-vis* the Accession was also distinctly more amenable to strengthening the relationship between the State and the Centre, and less charged with the Kashmiri chauvinism so sedulously fostered by Sheikh Abdullah.

Apart from the Jammu agitation, there was the broader question of implementing the 'Delhi Agreement' on the constitutional relationship between the State and the Centre that had been earlier worked out after prolonged negotiations between Sheikh Abdullah's team and representatives of the Government of India. While the decision regarding abolishing the monarchy had been rapidly implemented because it suited the Sheikh, he had begun dragging his feet as far as the other items were concerned. It had been clear to me from the start that he was less than sincere in his professions, and that he was simply manoeuvring himself into a position of strength in relation to the Central Government. Had he been sincere, why the delay in implementing the rest of the agreement?

In fact the Sheikh used one of his favourite techniques by initiating a debate within the National Conference Working Committee regarding the nature of the relationship with India. One group, led by M. A. Beg, was vociferous in its view that the relationship should not go beyond the three subjects contained in the Instrument of Accession, while the other, led by Bakshi Ghulam Mohammad and including G. L. Dogra and D. P. Dhar, was agreeable to a more comprehensive relationship covering other vital areas such as the judiciary, financial arrangements, and so on. This tussle within the National Conference gradually assumed serious dimensions. While the Sheikh ostensibly tried to keep himself above the controversy for some time, he increasingly began throwing his weight in favour of the hardliners. It was this development, even more than the Jammu agitation, that began to disturb Jawaharlal.

I had two long meetings with him on 21 April and 23 May. At the second meeting he opened up for the first time, and expressed his deep anguish at the way the situation in the State was developing. He admitted that he had no answer when asked in Parliament or outside as to why the Delhi Agreement had not been implemented. He said that he had written a long letter to the Sheikh pointing out that the matter had been greatly delayed and that, as he was going abroad in a few weeks, he would very much like to see the question finalized before he left. When I asked him what reply he had received he turned to me and said in an incredulous and hurt tone, 'I received no reply at all'. He added that the Sheikh was thoroughly confused and was evidently avoiding meeting him.

I mentioned that if the State Government made any move which showed that they were going back on their solemn agreements with the Government of India, my position would become impossible. It would be very difficult for me to continue to associate myself with them as I would never be a party to a betrayal of India. He pondered over that for a while but did not immediately respond. When I got up to leave he turned to me and said, 'Look here, one point I quite agree on is that if our agreements are thrown overboard or something like that, your position becomes absolutely impossible.' It was clear that he was deeply disturbed, but he had not quite made up his mind how to deal with the problem. He was particularly hurt, even bewildered, at the hostile manner in which his old protégé and friend Sheikh Abdullah was acting, and agreed with me when I remarked that unlimited power seemed to have brought out the Sheikh's worst fascist and totalitarian tendencies.

Indeed, the Sheikh's attitude steadily became more and more intransigent. He made a speech at Ranbirsinghpura, a border town near Jammu, where he reacted violently against the Jammu agitation, went on to accuse India of being communal and virtually threatening that the Accession of the State could not be taken for granted. I had been planning a visit to Europe, and had even written formally to the President and Jawaharlal about this, but in view of the growing tension following the Jammu agitation and the increasing schism within the National Conference I decided against going.

The annual move to Srinagar saw further deterioration. Dr Shyama Prasad Mukherjee, who had defied the ban on his entry to the State, had been arrested and kept in detention. On 10 June I sent a report to Jawaharlal, who was at that time on a fairly long visit to London, in which I said:

The political situation here in the valley continues to be extremely fluid. The division within the party is causing considerable tension. The pro-Indian faction continues to be determined, and claims to be strong and to have a majority both in the Working Committee and in the Assembly. Frequent meetings of the Working Committee continue.

I was shocked and astounded to gather from a private meeting with Sheikh Abdullah last week that he seems to have decided to go back upon the solemn agreements which he has concluded with India and upon his clear commitments. This cannot be allowed, as it will make our position absolutely impossible and be a grave blow to our National interests and naturally to our International position also. I need not mention the grave and widespread repercussions that will result from such a development. The problem will claim your immediate attention upon your return for a final and decisive solution.

Soon thereafter came the shocking news of the death of Dr Shyama Prasad Mukherjee in detention. I was not informed of his illness or his removal to hospital, and only learnt of his death from unofficial sources several hours after his body had been flown out of Srinagar. The circumstances in which he died in the custody of the State Government were a cause of grave resentment and suspicion. Jammu was furious because Dr Mukherjee had been martyred while fighting for the Praja Parishad cause, and there was open talk that his death had not been from natural causes. The whole of India was shocked at this event, specially the people of Bengal, who held Dr Mukherjee in the highest regard.

By now the Sheikh was clearly on the warpath. Despite repeated suggestions to visit Delhi, and an invitation from Jawaharlal to do so on 3 July, he refused to go down to the capital and discuss the whole situation. Maulana Azad came up to Srinagar for a few days, but instead of taking advantage of his visit to sort out differences, Sheikh Abdullah pointedly ignored him and he was virtually insulted by the National Conference workers. The Sheikh's speeches became more and more strident, and it become increasingly clear that he was seriously working on the idea of some sort of independent status for Kashmir which, inevitably, would imply a virtual negation of the Accession to India. At about this time Adlai Stevenson visited Srinagar and had long talks with the Sheikh. It is not known what exactly transpired, but the general impression was that in some way the Sheikh received encouragement from these conversations for his independence theory.

Meanwhile, the rift within the National Conference had come into the open. It was common knowledge that the Sheikh was favouring the hardliners led by M. A. Beg, while most of the other senior leaders, including the two Cabinet Ministers G. L. Dogra and Shamlal Saraf, and D. P. Dhar who was Deputy Minister, had rallied behind Bakshi Ghulam Mohammad. Bakshi came to my house on a few occasions in connection with meetings of the State Soldiers Board of which I was Chairman, and would stay on for a few minutes after the others had left. While I was careful not to give the impression of getting involved in the controversy, I had of course to maintain close contact with the pro-Indian group. D. P. Dhar was a frequent visitor, and he became one of the key figures in the drama that was about to unfold. Suave and unflappable, 'D.P.' had an incisive mind and was an excellent planner. He played a significant role in keeping New Delhi informed about the inner conflicts within the National Conference. Jawaharlal liked him and had regard for his political judgement.

It was at about this time that we began to realize that unless something drastic was done to curb Sheikh Abdullah, the situation would steadily deteriorate and finally get completely out of hand with grave and incalculable consequences for the entire country. The Kashmir issue was still a prominent item on the Security Council agenda, and it would be disastrous if the Sheikh, who had twice been sent to Lake Success as a member of the Indian delegation, were to do a volte-face while still Prime Minister of the State. I watched with increasing alarm and apprehension the trend of events, and decided that I should once more go down to Delhi and discuss the situation with Jawaharlal. This I did in the third week of July.

When I met him, I found Jawaharlal's attitude considerably changed. Not only did he not make any attempt to defend Sheikh Abdullah, he seemed to be as disturbed as I was about the way the situation was developing. It seems that, apart from my own letters, he had received detailed reports from the Intelligence Bureau (then headed by B. N. Mullick), D. P. Dhar and others from the State, as well as first-hand impressions from Maulana Azad and Jawaharlal's close political confidant, Rafi Ahmed Kidwai. He listened in grim silence to my detailed presentation, occasionally frowning and nodding agreement. I did not put any concrete proposal before him, but I did make it clear that if Sheikh Abdullah persisted in his hostile attitude a parting of the ways was inevitable. When I left he got up and saw me to the door. As I took leave he put his hand on my shoulder and said, 'Don't worry, do your best.'

Immediately upon my return to Srinagar I decided to break completely with the problem on hand and go off on a pilgrimage to Amarnath, the famous shrine dedicated to Lord Shiva and situated in a huge cave at an altitude of 13,000 feet. I had always wanted to go there, and felt that this was an appropriate time to do so. It would give me, hopefully, fresh strength to deal with the looming crisis. Also, as the trip would be well publicized, it would allay any suspicions that may have been raised by my airdash to Delhi. The main pilgrimage to Amarnath reaches the shrine on the full moon of Shravana, which falls sometime in August. However, some devotees go a month earlier, and the July full moon was on the 26th. We therefore left Srinagar on the 23rd.

The trip was one of the most memorable I have ever made. From Pahalgam I was carried in a *dandy*, as my leg was still not good enough to manage the steep climbs, while Asha insisted on walking all the way. We camped for three nights—at Chandanwari, Sheshnag and Panchtarni—before reaching the famous cave. The scenery *en route* was breathtaking, specially the fabulous milky-green Sheshnag lake set against a massive, triple-peaked glacier. Once again I was struck by the uplifting power of natural beauty, particularly in the higher altitudes. As I wrote in a series of articles published by the *Hindustan Times* in its Sunday supplements:

One distinctly feels the presence of a Power greater, stronger and purer than one's own petty self. For a while I glimpse the lovely face of nature in its pure undesecrated majesty. The torrent of time slackens, the problems and strifes of life pale into insignificance and I am lost in deep contemplation. I cherish a desire in the recesses of my heart to one day build myself a small Ashrama in such surroundings where, with the body and mind made pure and free from the tentacles of desire and fear, ego and attachment, one can concentrate upon the unalloyed purity of Nature and thereby perhaps achieve spiritual illumination.

These articles were subsequently published in a small booklet called *The Glory of Amarnath*, which was my first literary endeavour.

The cave itself was much bigger than I had imagined, and in one corner stood the glistening ice formation about five feet high, symbolizing the creative energy of Lord Shiva. The shrine is unique in that the ice *lingam* forms of itself every year, and is believed to wax and wane with the moon. On the journey I was reading Paul Brunton's *Search in Secret India*, and the whole experience made a deep impression upon me. I have found repeatedly that an outer crisis is an excellent time to deepen one's inner aspiration, that the thicker the battle presses the more significant becomes the voice of the inner charioteer.

I returned to Srinagar on 28 July. During my absence there had been a fresh series of meetings of the National Conference Working Committee at which the two sides had clashed— Sheikh Abdullah was now openly partisan in the controversy, but only one other member of his Cabinet, M. A. Beg, supported him. The rift in the Cabinet came to a head on 7 August when the Sheikh, using a flimsy pretext, decided to move against the opposing group by asking for the resignation of Pandit Sham Lal Saraf. On the 8th morning Saraf sent me a copy of a long letter to the Sheikh in which he accused him of having repudiated the declared policies of the National Conference concerning the relationship of the State with the Indian Union. He refused to resign saying that 'the manner in which you have created a dangerous situation in the country by making highly inflammable speeches before the public, combined with your authoritarian attitude in the Cabinet, have convinced me that instead of helping the difficult situation my

resignation will encourage you to pursue your policies un-
bridled. Such a course will be suicidal for the country.'

A few hours later I received a signed copy of a memorandum
sent to Sheikh Abdullah by the Deputy Prime Minister, Bakshi
Ghulam Mohammad, the Finance Minister, G. L. Dogra and
the Health Minister, Pandit Sham Lal Saraf. The five-page
document squarely accused the Sheikh and M. A. Beg of
blatantly flouting accepted party policies. It said:

After convening of the Constituent Assembly, certain inescapable
elaborations of the State's relationship with India were defined in the
Delhi Agreement, of which you were the Chief architect on our
behalf. Your stand was unanimously endorsed by the Government,
the National Conference, the Indian Parliament and the Constituent
Assembly of the State. But you have not only deliberately delayed the
implementation of the Agreements on these matters, which form the
sheet-anchor of our policy, but have purposefully and openly de-
nounced these in public. You have thus arbitrarily sought to precipitate a rupture in the relationship of the State with India.

They added:

Mr M. A. Beg has persistently been following policies of narrow
sectarianism and communalism, which have seriously undermined the
oneness of the State. Unfortunately, you have been lending your
support to his policies in the Cabinet and his activities in public. This
has generated bitter feelings of suspicion and doubt in the minds of the
people of the various constituent units of the State. You have connived
at all these unfortunate happenings and thus strengthened and en-
couraged the forces of disruption. The result is that unity and secular
character, the two fundamental aspects of our State, stand threatened
today.

Concluding, the three Ministers said:

We have been constantly urging upon you to put an end to these un-
healthy tendencies and to undertake unitedly measures for restoring
the morale of the people. In spite of our best intentions, we have failed
in our efforts. It is, therefore, with great pain that we have to inform
you of our conclusion that the Cabinet, constituted as it is at present
and lacking as it does the unity of purpose and action, has lost the
confidence of the people in its ability to give them a clean, efficient and
healthy administration.

As soon as I received this communication, which was not
entirely unexpected, the ball was squarely in my court. Legally

the Council of Ministers held office at the pleasure of the Sadar-i-Riyasat, and as the appointing authority I also enjoyed the power of dismissal, even if this was not specifically spelt out. However, before taking any drastic action, I thought it was only appropriate that I should talk with Sheikh Abdullah. I immediately invited him to come across to see me as soon as possible. He was going to Gulmarg that afternoon, and came to my residence around noon. When I inquired about the situation he narrated three long though petty incidents regarding Shamlal Saraf, and disclosed that he had asked him to resign. He mentioned that the Kashmir Trade Commissioner in Delhi had telephoned him in the morning and informed him that the newspapers carried big headlines about the 'constitutional crisis' in Kashmir, and expressed surprise at the leak.

I said that I was deeply distressed and concerned at the recent trend of events, particularly the complete absence of homogeneity in the Cabinet. I pointed out that it would be useful if he and his Cabinet colleagues were to come to my residence that evening so that the whole matter could be discussed in depth. He sidetracked this suggestion by launching into an angry tirade against the Indian Press which he accused of grossly misrepresenting and exaggerating the differences in the Cabinet. He made the astonishing claim that, although there was some difference of opinion, there were no basic political or administrative differences within his Cabinet. When I again stressed the necessity of doing something to rectify the situation he stated quite clearly that no internal solution was possible until there was some external solution acceptable to India as well as Pakistan.

This revealed his true state of mind. From a position of clearly endorsing the Accession to India as 'final and irrevocable', he had over the last few months moved into an entirely different posture. He was evidently expecting some international pressure to be brought upon India to grant virtual independent status to Kashmir, and this was quite obviously the reason why he was holding up the implementation of the Delhi Agreement which would further cement the relationship between the State and the Centre. In our meeting he was not only unable to give me any assurance that the internal crisis in his Cabinet would be resolved, but had added a new dimension of uncertainty by talking about an 'external solution'.

Our meeting lasted for about forty-five minutes, after which he left saying that he was going to Gulmarg for the weekend. It was quite clear to me that something had to be done at once if further drift was to be avoided. I summoned my political and legal advisers, including D. P. Dhar and Brigadier (later General) B. M. Kaul, who was acting as a sort of unofficial courier between us and Delhi. The Sheikh was still a popular figure in the valley despite the fact that corruption and mal-administration had to some extent eroded his stature. If we gave him an opportunity to take his case to the streets he would easily arouse acute communal and chauvinistic sentiments among the Kashmiri masses, which could in turn result in serious and violent disturbances. Anti-national elements and agents were active in the valley and, if given the chance, would not hesitate to plunge the State into utter turmoil. Parliament was in session, and anything happening here would at once have its repercussions on the national scene.

We, therefore, decided that the Sheikh would have to be dismissed. While I was reluctant that he should be arrested, Bakshi Ghulam Mohammad made it quite clear that he could not undertake to run the Government if the Sheikh and Beg were left free to propagate their views. Dismissing and detaining a sitting Prime Minister was no easy task, as all plans had to be made in absolute secrecy. The police had to be organized, the Indian Army kept discreetly informed, and the media handled in an imaginative manner. Luckily, D. P. Dhar was a superb tactician who was at his best in such situations. In the three days preceding the crisis 'D.P.', who was Deputy Home Minister, had tied up all these details.

The fact that the Sheikh decided to go up to Gulmarg, however, necessitated some last minute change of plans. Soon after he left my house we sat down to draft the dismissal order. Along with this I dictated a covering letter to Sheikh Abdullah. The text of these documents was as follows:

SECRET

Karan Mahal,
Srinagar
August 8, 1953.

My dear Sheikh Abdullah,

You will recall that in the course of our meeting today I conveyed to you my deep concern at the serious differences which exist in your

11

Cabinet. I impressed upon you the immediate necessity for restoring harmony and unity of purpose among the members of the Cabinet in the execution of its policies. You were, however, unable to assure me that these acute differences could be remedied.

This conflict within the Cabinet has for a considerable time been causing great confusion and apprehension in the minds of the people of the State. The situation has reached an unprecedented crisis with the fact that three of your four Cabinet colleagues have in a Memorandum to you, a copy of which they have sent to me, expressed their complete dissatisfaction with your actions and policies, which have lost the present Cabinet the confidence of the people. This document clearly indicates that the divergence within your Cabinet has reached proportions in which the unity, prosperity and stability of the State are gravely jeopardized.

When we met today I further suggested to you that an emergent meeting of the Cabinet should be held at my residence this evening so that we could jointly explore the possibilities of securing a stable, unified and efficient Government for the country. But to my regret you evaded the issue.

Under these conditions I, as Head of the State, have been forced to the conclusion that the present Cabinet cannot continue in office any longer and hence I regret to inform you that I have dissolved the Council of Ministers headed by you. A copy of my order in this connection is attached herewith.

I need hardly add how deeply distressed I am at having to take this action, but the vital interests of the people of the State, which it is my duty to safeguard, leave me no alternative. I trust that this will in no way affect the mutual regard and cordial feelings we have for each other.

Yours sincerely,
Karan Singh
Sadar-i-Riyasat

ORDER

Whereas for some months I have been noticing with growing concern that there have existed acute differences of opinion between members of the Government on basic issues—political, economic and administrative—affecting the vital interests of the State;

And whereas members of the Government have been publicly expressing sharply conflicting points of view regarding these matters;

And whereas on these fundamental issues the views of a majority of the members of the Cabinet are sharply opposed to the view held by the Prime Minister and one of his colleagues;

And whereas efforts to work in harmony and pull together as a team having failed, and the majority in the Cabinet has expressed that, lacking as it does in unity of purpose and action, the present Cabinet has lost the confidence of the people;

And whereas the economic distress of the people has considerably increased which needs prompt and serious attention;

And whereas a stage has reached in which the very process of honest and efficient administration has become impracticable;

And whereas, finally, the functioning of the present Cabinet on the basis of joint responsibility has become impossible and the resultant conflicts have gravely jeopardized the unity, prosperity and stability of the State;

I, Karan Singh, Sadar-i-Riyasat, functioning in the interests of the people of the State who have reposed the responsibility and authority of the Headship of the State in me, do hereby dismiss Sheikh Mohammad Abdullah from the Prime Ministership of the State of Jammu and Kashmir, and consequently the Council of Ministers headed by him is dissolved forthwith.

SADAR-I-RIYASAT
JAMMU & KASHMIR

Srinagar,
August 8, 1953

By the time the documents were ready it was late evening. The weather was also in a turbulent mood; it was pouring, thunder rumbled and jagged shafts of lightning cut through the clouds. I deputed my ADC, Major B. S. Bajwa, to go to Gulmarg and deliver the letter to Sheikh Abdullah. A police party also went along with him, but they were delayed by the torrential rain and the bad road beyond Tangmarg. Having dispatched the documents we all waited in Karan Mahal for word that they had been delivered. As this was delayed, tension grew. Our gamble was a risky one, for if the Sheikh got even an inkling of what was happening he would react ferociously, and our own lives may well have been in danger. However, the die was cast, and all we could do was to pray that the whole operation went off smoothly.

As it turned out, our prayers were answered. The Sheikh was totally unaware of the developments, and so arrogant in the possession of power that he could never dream that anyone would dare to challenge him. When the ADC and the police contingent finally reached Gulmarg it was late at night, and the

11A

Sheikh and Begum Abdullah were fast asleep. With some difficulty and much knocking he was awoken and handed the
letter as well as a warrant of arrest. On reading it he flew into a
rage and shouted, 'Who is the Sadar-i-Riyasat to dismiss me?
I made that chit of a boy Sadar-i-Riyasat.' But by then his house
was fully surrounded by the police. He was given two hours to
say his *namaz* and pack, during which we later learnt he burnt a
number of documents that he had with him. This could have
been prevented, but we had given strict instructions to the
police that he and the Begum were to be treated with courtesy
and not physically harassed in any way. In the early hours of
the 9th morning they were escorted to a car and driven out of
the valley to the Tara Niwas guest house in Udhampur, where
they were kept in detention. M. A. Beg and several others were
also arrested that night in Srinagar and other parts of the valley.

Meanwhile, it was my responsibility to see that there was no
constitutional gap in the administration of the State. With the
dismissal of Sheikh Abdullah I wrote to Bakshi Ghulam
Mohammad inviting him to meet me and discuss the formation
of the new Government. I ended the letter by saying that 'the
continuance in office of the new Cabinet will depend upon its
securing a vote of confidence from the Legislative Assembly
during its coming session'. Bakshi came over and we discussed
the situation. I felt that no time should be lost in swearing in the
new Government. We summoned the Chief Secretary, M. K.
Kidwai, who was blissfully unaware of what was happening.
When he learnt that the Sheikh had been dismissed and arrested
he sank down on the steps holding his head in his hands, and
was revived only after he had been plied with a couple of stiff
whiskies.

In the early hours of 9 August I administered the oath of
office to Bakshi Ghulam Mohammad and G. L. Dogra, so that
they would be in a position to deal with the tense situation that
would inevitably develop as soon as the news of the dismissal
and arrests spread in the valley. I then wrote a report to the
President informing him of the entire developments, and sent a
copy to Jawaharlal with a covering letter which included these
two paragraphs:

We are all acutely aware of the gravity of the step that we have been
forced to take and also of the extent of its possible repercussions, both

within and without the State. In this whole matter I have attempted to act in a democratic and constitutional manner, keeping especially in mind what you said when we met last. On the whole I feel that we have done the best that was possible under the circumstances.

Regarding what was to be done with Sheikh Abdullah after his dismissal, this was of course a decision for the new Government to take. On my part I strongly urged them to desist from arresting him soon after the dismissal, but they were most apprehensive that with his presence in the valley at this juncture reactions would have been greatly intensified and there was a grave danger of the situation getting completely out of hand and even resulting in violence and bloodshed. Consequently he has been arrested this morning at Gulmarg and is being taken to Udhampur where he will be lodged in the State Guest House. I have stressed that he and his family be accorded all courtesy and consideration.

By the time the whole operation was over dawn had broken. The clouds and thunder of the last two days had disappeared, and the sky was clear again. I got through to Jawaharlal on the telephone just before eight but the line was unclear. In its morning bulletin All India Radio devoted thirteen of its fifteen minutes to a detailed report on the developments in Kashmir. I had not slept a wink that night and found myself in a curiously detached and light-headed mood. I knew that what I had done was for the national good, and that all the danger and risks were worth taking if it served the country. Asha had also sat up anxiously in her room all night. Slowly I climbed up the steps and walked into her room. 'It is over', I said, and we both smiled; she sixteen going on seventeen, I twenty-two going on twenty-three. I was asleep almost before I hit the bed.

Index